HORRIBLE
CHRISTMAS

Terry Deary ✷ Martin Brown

SCHOLASTIC
PRESS

This book is for John Goddard,
Lincolnshire's answer to everything. TD

To my mum. MB

A division of Scholastic UK Ltd
London ~ New York ~ Toronto ~ Sydney ~ Auckland
Mexico City ~ New Delhi ~ Hong Kong

First published in the UK by Scholastic Ltd, 2000
This edition published 2005

Text copyright © Terry Deary, 2000
Illustrations copyright © Martin Brown, 2000
Colour by Atholl McDonald
Crackers Christmas CD: Text © Terry Deary 2000,
2005 recording © and ℗ Testbed Productions and Scholastic UK Ltd.

www.testbed.co.uk

"Grandma Got Run Over By A Reindeer" written by Randy Brooks © copyright 1979.
Kris Publishing and Elmo Publishing (both admin. by ICG).
All rights reserved. Used by permission.

ISBN 0 439 95459 2

CONTENTS

 CRACKERS CHRISTMAS CD

1. Terry's terrible Christmas
2. The first Christmas
3. Curious carols
4. The holy innocents
5. The real Santa Claus
6. The day they banned Christmas
7. How Dickens made Christmas
8. Music hall misery
9. Crackers Christmas
10. The Sedgefield spook
11. Putrid panto

Remember to keep your **FREE CD** handy as you read...

INTRODUCTION

In the words of the delightful Mr Scrooge in Charles Dickens's *A Christmas Carol* …

Bah! Humbug! Merry Christmas? Out upon Merry Christmas! What's Christmas time to you but a time for paying bills without money? A time for finding yourself a year older and not an hour richer?

He's right, of course. When it comes to this Christmas a lot of people haven't finished paying for *last* Christmas! One day of burnt turkey and shrivelled pudding in return for three hundred and sixty-four days of debt. Bah! Humbug!

What was the charming Scrooge's answer? Simple. You may like to try it …

Every idiot who goes around with 'Merry Christmas' on his lips should be boiled with his own pudding…

It may be a bit tricky getting a pot big enough and then getting the 'idiot' into the pot. The trouble with boiling idiots in the pudding pot is that it

 LISTEN TO 'TERRY'S TERRIBLE CHRISTMAS', 'HOW DICKENS MADE CHRISTMAS' AND 'MUSIC HALL MISERY' ON YOUR CD!

ruins the taste of the pudding. Never mind, Mr Scrooge tells you what to do when the Christmas idiot has been boiled to death …

He should be buried with a stake of holly through his heart. He should!

Sadly Mr Scrooge turns out to be a kind and giving old wrinklie under all that tough talk. He changes!

But some sensible people would like to keep the *old* Scrooge spirit alive. They'd like to set fire to all Christmas puddings and stick them up the pudding-cooks' noses. They'd love to put all the terrible presents in a pit and cover them with reindeer droppings …

Those people need some really good excuses to be cruel at Christmas. They need a book filled full of the foulest facts you can find on this festive folly! So next time someone wishes them a 'Happy Christmas' they can stuff them like a turkey with the truth about this sick and silly season!

To be the new Scrooge of the 21st century they need a horrible history of Christmas. And here it is …

THANKS !…BAH! HUMBUG!

CHRISTMAS CAROLS

Bothered by carol singers – croaking old crows or begging brats? What can you say to make them stop?

TELL THEM CAROLS AREN'T A CHRISTMASSY THING TO SING! SAY 'HANG ON CAROL SINGERS...'

Good King Wenceslas looked out ...

'Wenceslas was a duke, not a king. Wenceslas I of Bohemia was NOT famous for collecting firewood for oldies too decrepit to pick their own. That was just a story made up in the 1800s to fit an old tune from the 1300s.'

In AD 929 Wenceslas spread Christianity through Bohemia. This annoyed his mother and his brother who met him at a church door and chopped Wenceslas to pieces. Wence was only 22 years old. He didn't do a lot of gathering winter's fuel after that. And, by the way, the feast of Stephen is 26 December.

Away in a manger, no crib for a bed ...

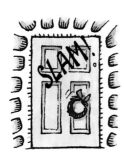

'Jesus was NOT born in a stable. He was born in a cave. That's because Joseph's first wife and their six kids made his house too crowded!'

 LISTEN TO 'CURIOUS CAROLS' ON YOUR FREE CD!

At least that's what Irish monk Father Jerome O'Connor reckons. And he's one of the world's top Bible archaeologists. And in Saint Matthew's story in the Bible, Jesus was born in a house.

Hark the herald angels sing …

'There were NO singing angels around when Jesus was born. The reporters wrote in Greek of 'angelos' being there … but that's not Greek for 'angels', it's Greek for 'messenger'.'

Joseph and Mary had their baby and there were shepherd friends in the area, looking after their sheep. The 'angelos' were probably kids who shouted up to their dads on the hillsides, 'Oi, Dad! Joseph and Mary have had their baby! It's a boy!'

Father Jerome O'Connor again. Clever feller, isn't he?

We three kings of Orient are …

'They were NOT 'kings', just wise men. And how do you know there were three? There could have been a dozen or more!'

The Bible says:

> Jesus was born in the town of Bethlehem in Judea, during the time when Herod was king. Soon afterwards, some men who studied the stars came from the east to Jerusalem and asked 'Where is the baby born to be the king of the Jews? We saw his star when it came up in the east, and we have come to worship him.'

Yes, all right, three *gifts* are mentioned … gold, frankincense and myrrh … and that's why painters in the Middle Ages showed three wise men – one gift each. But there could have been a few other wise blokes there who used all their gold getting their camels into the multi-storey camel park.

Here we come a wassailing …

'A wassail was just a pagan excuse for awful adults to get drunk as a skunk. It had nothing to do with Christmas or the birth of Jesus!'

Wassail was a drink of ale, nutmeg, honey and ginger. Wassailers arrive at a house at Christmas and the owner must offer them the drink. He must say 'Waes hael' – old English for 'Be healthy!' The wassailers reply 'Drinc hael' – 'Drink and be healthy'.

To make the wassail drink more chewy there should be pieces of toast floating on top. The wassail bowl is passed round; the first guest takes out a piece of toast and wishes everyone good health. (That's where we get the idea of 'drink a toast' to someone today.) Then everyone drinks and moves on to the next house to scrounge some more. Wassailing? Hah!

Did you Noel …?

The carol 'Silent Night' was first played on a guitar. It was supposed to be played on a church organ in Austria. But the organ was powered by a fellow on a bellows and mice had chewed through the bellows. (They probably wanted a silent night's sleep.) A guitar had to be used instead. (There's another story that some nasty human deliberately wrecked the bellows, but the mice story is nice.)

Cool carols

If you are going carol singing then liven things up with these versions …

Good king Senseless last looked out
On the feast of Stephen.
A snowball gave his ear a clout,
He cried, 'I will get even!'

Or …

> We three kings of Orient are,
> One in a taxi, one in a car,
> One on a scooter blowing his hooter,
> Smoking a big cigar.

Or …

> While shepherds washed their socks by night
> All watching ITV,
> The angel of the Lord came down
> And switched to BBC.

Did you Noel …?

The reason why carol singers knock on your door and pester you when you're trying to watch your favourite Christmas soap on television is because they were once banned from churches!

The word 'carol' is from a Greek word meaning 'sing and dance in a circle'. The medieval priests were upset by carol singers who danced through their churches at Christmas. The priests claimed the carol singers were doing the work of the devil and threw them out. So the warbling wasters went round houses instead … and they still do.

Sick songs
Or of course you could sing anti-Christmas songs like this American hit, written in 1977 by Randy Brooks …

GRANDMA GOT RUN OVER BY A REINDEER

Grandma got run over by a reindeer
Walking home from our house Christmas Eve.
You can say there's no such thing as Santa,
But as for me an' Grandpa, we believe.

When we found her Christmas morning,
At the scene of the attack,
She had hoof-prints on her forehead,
And incriminating Claus marks on her back.

It's not Christmas without Grandma,
All the family's dressed in black.
And we just can't help but wonder,
Should we open up her gifts or give them back?

I've warned all my friends and neighbours,
Better watch out for your selves.
They should never give a licence,
To a man who drives a sleigh and plays with elves!

CHRISTMAS HISTORY

People say Christmas is a 'tradition'. We've always done it! But that's just not true. Tell them the truth!

6 BC   Jesus is born (probably), six years before the birth of Christ! He was born when the Romans were doing a census counting all the people in their empire, wasn't he? (That's how Mary and Joseph ended up in Bethlehem with no room at the pub.) The Romans only did that check once every 14 years – so he could have been born in 20 BC, 6 BC or AD 8. The historians' favourite is 6 BC.

AD 313 Constantine becomes the first Christian Roman Emperor. The Romans already had wild parties at the end of December to celebrate the days getting longer again. 25 December was the sun's birthday and the parties were mega. The Christians pinched that party date to celebrate the birth of Jesus ... even though that wasn't his birthday. The Romans didn't mind. They still had an excuse to get drunk.

440   People have been celebrating the birth of Jesus in January and March as well as December. In 440 the Church in Rome fixes it at 25 December. Churches are worried that people are enjoying Christmas in the old Roman sun-god way – eating, boozing and dancing around in animal skins or other weird costumes.

1038   'Cristes Maesse' written in a Saxon book – the first record we have of 'Christmas' in writing.

 LISTEN TO 'THE FIRST CHRISTMAS' ON YOUR FREE CD!

1066 William the Conqueror has himself crowned at Westminster Abbey on Christmas Day. The lords inside give a mighty cheer – the guards outside think there's a rebellion going on. They attack and burn down houses in the area. Not very merry Christmas.

1519 The turkey finally arrives in Europe. Good news for Christmas eaters ... bad news for the turkeys.

1541 Henry VIII's Unlawful Games Act bans every kind of sport on a Christmas Day ... except archery because English men should be ready to go into battle at any time with the foul French or the savage Scots. So, you can't have a timid game of tennis but you can practise murdering someone with a blood-letting bow! As time went on people pleaded to have their favourite sports on Christmas Day but most of these requests were turned down. The only one that was allowed was 'leaping and vaulting'.

1647 Christmas abolished in Britain. Oliver Cromwell and his Puritan Parliament passed a law to ban it – 25 December was to be a working day and Parliament met every Christmas from 1644 to 1656. There were riots across the country. Christmas church services were broken up by armed soldiers. Shopkeepers came off worst – if they closed then soldiers forced them to open ... and if they opened then rioters forced them to close! Christmas decorations in London were torn down and burned by the mayor. (Probably at night because he sounds a bit of a night-mayor.) Christmas  puddings were banned. You weren't allowed to make them – so people just ordered them from Europe. The unhappy people got together a petition and said: 'If we could not have our Christmas Day, we would have the king back on his throne.' Fighting Christmas talk!

 LISTEN TO 'THE DAY THEY BANNED CHRISTMAS' ON YOUR FREE CD!

1659 In America the Puritan leaders banned Christmas in some states. A New England state law said: 'Whosoever shall be found observing any such day as Christmas shall pay five shillings as a fine.' And you could buy a lot of stuffing for five shillings! Other states, like Virginia, did not ban Christmas and they were probably the first to eat turkey for Christmas dinner. The ban-Christmas laws were dropped in 1681 but it wasn't until 1836 that Alabama said 25 December was to be a holiday, and then everyone in the USA copied them.

1660 Christmas is back in Britain. The writer Samuel Pepys says he went to church where the priest was whingeing on, 'People are having happy Christmas parties and forgetting that it is really a religious day.' Nothing much changes then.

1790s People begin to lose interest in Christmas. They think it's a bit silly and old fashioned.

1843 Charles Dickens publishes *A Christmas Carol* and suddenly Victorian Britain decides Christmas is a wonderful idea.

1914 The first Christmas of the First World War and football breaks out. German and British enemies meet on frozen ground between their trenches and play a Christmas game of footie. The two sides sing carols to one another on Christmas Eve. They have a shooting contest, shooting at tin cans instead of each other. Brits swap their Christmas puddings for barrels of German beer. Germans put up trees lit with candles in their trenches. Enemies meet in the middle of the battle area and exchange addresses, promising to write to one another after the war. The generals (who probably preferred posh rugby and cricket) say that soldiers will be shot if they don't start shooting bullets instead of balls.

 # CHRISTMAS CRACKERS

The crackers man

Ever wondered who invented Christmas crackers? Here's one story …

A young man called Tom Smith owned, and worked in, a sweet shop in London. Tom sold sugared almonds, each one wrapped in bright paper, like the French ones. They sold well and he noticed that young men were buying them to give to their sweethearts. He began placing 'love mottoes' on small slips of paper inside the sweet wrapping. You know the sort of thing, 'I think you are as gorgeous as a pint of beer' or 'Will you marry me and do my washing and ironing?'

In 1846 Tom began to wonder if he could cash in on Christmas. Instead of sweets, why not wrap little toys and novelties in the twisted wrapping? Tom experimented and had the idea of making a wrapping that could be pulled apart. The Christmas toy-in-a-pull-apart-wrapper was a success, but Tom was still not satisfied.

One evening he was standing in front of the fire when he kicked his Christmas log into place. There was a shower of sparks and the log crackled and almost set Tom's trousers on fire.

'That's it!' Tom cried. 'What I need is something in my wrapping that will make a "crack" when it is pulled open.'

He worked with several chemicals until at last he found one that was safe, easy to make, and would make a noise just loud enough to amuse his customers and not scare the pants off them.

The new 'crackers' were a huge success, and Tom had to open a factory to produce them and he lived happily ever after.

 LISTEN TO 'CRACKERS CHRISTMAS' ON YOUR FREE CD!

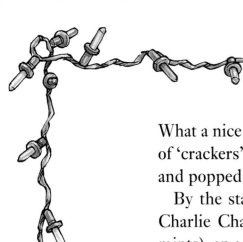

What a nice story! Who told the story? Tom Smith! But there is mention of 'crackers' in a story published in 1841 – five years before Tom snapped and popped into history. So was Tom a fibber? Who knows?

By the start of the 1900s crackers were packed in 'theme' boxes – a Charlie Chaplin set, an Arctic Exploration set (probably full of polar mints), an aeroplane set (they probably flew off the shelves), a cinema set (probably with no snap in them as they were silent movies in those days) and even a set for Leap Year – the year when women can propose marriage to men – which had rings and fake marriage certificates inside.

The world's worst jokes

We should all be grateful to old Tom for crackers, except for one thing … he had the idea of putting jokes in the crackers. And they are usually the worst, cringe-making jokes in the history of the world!

Here are two cracker jokes from Victorian times …

Q. WHAT IS A FISHERMAN'S FAVOURITE MUSICAL INSTRUMENT?
A. A CAST-A-NET!

Q. WHAT DO YOU GIVE A DEAF FISHERMAN?
A. A HERRING AID!

(You will find this sort of joke scattered throughout the book. The publishers take no blame for these jokes that are about as funny as a slap on the ear with a wet kipper.)

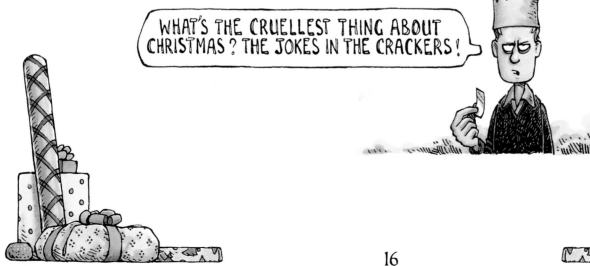

WHAT'S THE CRUELLEST THING ABOUT CHRISTMAS? THE JOKES IN THE CRACKERS!

CHRISTMAS KIDS

Christmas crib

Lots of schools and shops and city centres have models of a stable with Joseph, Mary, three wise men, shepherds and their animals. But the first time the Nativity scene was copied they used *live* animals ... and a live saint who played all the parts except baby Jesus!

In 1223 Saint Francis of Assisi in Italy wanted to find a way to tell the local people the Christmas story. So he set up a crib in a cave on the mountainside with live animals and a wooden doll for Jesus. He then acted as shepherds, kings, angels and so on. A sort of one-man Christmas show.

It was a smash hit and he had to repeat it every Christmas. He decided to bring in a second actor to play one of the roles. Which one?

a) A talking lonely lamb   **b)** The baby Jesus   **c)** Mary

> *Answer:*
> **b)** Saint Francis used a real baby. When the crib babies grew up they were always treated well, so he chose orphans from the local children's home.

Years later, the king of Naples, in Italy, made figures for a Christmas crib himself, and the queen and court ladies dressed them. In other years, the king paid famous artists and sculptors to make wonderful new figures.

Gradually the custom spread to other countries – especially to France, Spain, Portugal and southern Germany. Since the days of Saint Francis some of the cribs have been a bit odd …

- In Munich, after a heavy fall of snow at Christmas time, a snow-crib is built.
- There is a permanent underwater crib in Amalfi, in Italy, where life-size figures have been placed in the form of a Nativity scene on the sea bed.
- At a special exhibition of cribs in France in 1966, a 'space crib' was set up. The Nativity scene was set on a distant planet, and the three wise men were shown arriving in a rocket!

The animals

Talking about cribs, where did the idea of the animals come from? Is it in the Bible? No. Animals are not mentioned in the Bible stories about Christmas.

It all started twelve hundred years after the birth of Christ when a carol described how the donkey carried Mary to Bethlehem and the other animals looked after her and the new baby in the stable. The cow gave her the manger for a bed and hay for a pillow and warmed the baby Jesus with her breath. (Have you ever smelt a cow's breath? Phew! What a way to be warmed to sleep! An electric blanket is better every time. Still, it was very kind of the cow who must have got a bit peckish.) The sheep gave her wool for a blanket and the doves cooed him to sleep.

On that first Christmas night, a legend says, the animals and birds talked about the wonderful news. People said they spoke in Latin, of course, because that was the language used in church.

Can you work out which animal spoke which words? (The clue is in the sound!) The conversation went like this …

1) Christus natus est! (Christ is born!)   a) the sheep
2) Ubi? (Where?)   b) the cockerel
3) Bethlehem   c) the ox

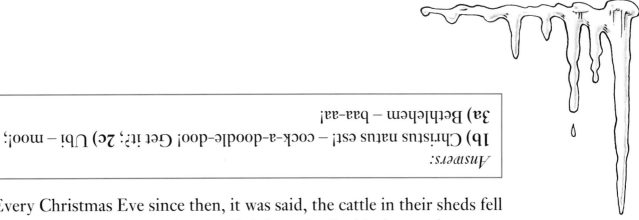
Every Christmas Eve since then, it was said, the cattle in their sheds fell on their knees at the stroke of midnight and talked in human language. Humans couldn't listen in though. Shame. It could have been interesting.

Bees gathered in their hive and hummed the Hundredth Psalm – why did they hum it? Maybe they didn't know the words. But never try to listen to any of them! It was said to be very unlucky!

The baby bath

For over a thousand years painters have shown the scene of the birth of Jesus. Until the 1500s these paintings often showed baby Jesus having his first bath. Then, in the middle of the 1500s, a meeting of priests *banned* pictures of Jesus in the bath! Why?

  a) The baby Jesus had no clothes on and they thought it was a bit rude.

  b) Jesus was so pure he would never have needed a bath.

  c) Baths hadn't been invented when Jesus was born so it was a daft thing to show.

19

Answer:
b) The meeting was called 'The Council of Trent' and lasted from 1545 till 1563, which is an awful lot of talking!

Christmas star

You may have heard that a star appeared in the sky over Bethlehem and guided the wise men to a stable where Jesus was born. If that's true then it was a true miracle – God made a star, although it might have been easier to make a map book with an arrow saying, 'This way, lads!'

Astronomers say there were no comets around the time of Christ's birth. But if he was born in 6 BC then three large planets – Mars, Jupiter and Saturn – were close together in a triangle. *That* could have been the strange sign that got the wise men going.

Did you Noel ... ?

It's a bit rough being born on Christmas Day – you get all your presents at once and you have to share your party with the world – but there is one good thing about it. An old superstition says ...

Those who are born on Christmas Day cannot see spirits.

AAAAH!

WHAT?

So anyone born on Christmas Day can happily spend the night in a graveyard and have a peaceful night's sleep, except for the sound of the worms munching away at the bodies, of corpse.

Funeral frankincense

You can understand why the three wise men brought gold for the baby Jesus. But what were these frankincense and myrrh things? They were very rare types of 'gum' from trees. They were as valuable as gold and made pleasant perfumes in the days when people could be very smelly.

The Romans used frankincense for their funerals. How?

a) They burned it with the bodies at funerals.

b) They dressed the corpse of a dead friend with perfumed robes.

c) They put it in the coffin so the corpse would have riches in the afterlife.

Answer:
a) The smell of cremated human flesh was so horrible they burned frankincense to make it more pleasant.

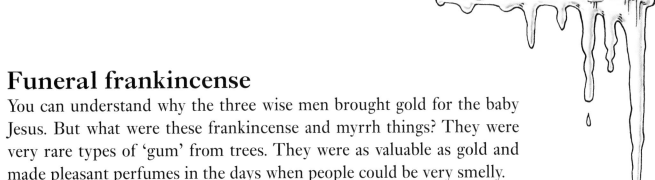

Q. WHAT'S THE BEST EVER CHRISTMAS PRESENT?
A. A BROKEN DRUM, COS YOU CAN'T BEAT IT!

Childermass Day

Not everybody was happy at the thought of a baby born in Bethlehem …

'He's born to be king!' some happy people said.

'He can't be,' King Herod said. 'I'm king! This town's too small for the two of us.'

'What can you do?' they asked him.

'A king's gotta do what a king's gotta do. I'll murder the little feller!'

'But you don't know what he looks like!' his councillors argued. 'We haven't got his picture 'cos cameras haven't been invented. Anyway the little horrors all look the same when they're a couple of days old!'

Herod had a horrible leer on his face (probably) as he said, 'So

 LISTEN TO 'THE HOLY INNOCENTS' ON YOUR FREE CD!

21

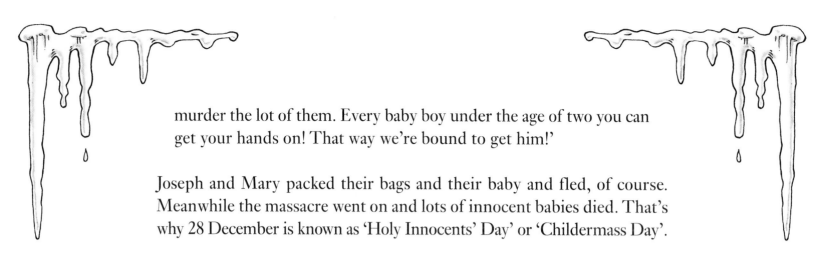

murder the lot of them. Every baby boy under the age of two you can get your hands on! That way we're bound to get him!'

Joseph and Mary packed their bags and their baby and fled, of course. Meanwhile the massacre went on and lots of innocent babies died. That's why 28 December is known as 'Holy Innocents' Day' or 'Childermass Day'.

What you should tell adults

In some parts of Europe Childermass Day was celebrated by choosing a boy to be bishop for the day. He and his friends were in charge. (What would you do if you were top tot of the town?) The lads were showered with presents.

The custom died out in the 1600s … but you may want to see it revived!

HIS HOLINESS DEMANDS MORE SWEETIES

What you mustn't tell adults!

28 December has been called an unlucky day. In many countries no one would marry on that day, and no one would start a new building. Edward IV of England even refused to be crowned on that day.

There was an old English custom that died out in the middle of the 1700s. Children had to be reminded of Herod's cruelty. So children were *beaten*. Some adults (especially teachers) may well enjoy seeing this custom revived! Better not tell them about it, eh?!

DAFT DATA

Christmas is a time of enormous eating and stupendous spending. Can you work out the right answers to these excessive Xmas facts?

1. Put them end to end and they'd stretch from the Tower of London to the pyramids of Egypt. What?
a) The mince pies we eat every Christmas.
b) The £20 notes taken from bank tills on a Christmas shopping day.
c) The fir trees we murder for Christmas trees.

2. The British Isles could sink under the extra 158,000 tonnes we put on them every Christmas. Tonnes of what?
a) Tinsel
b) Human fat
c) Christmas party crisps

3. British people buy 1.6 billion of them every year. What?
a) Christmas cards
b) Christmas tree lights
c) Plastic Sledges

BUT I WANT A YELLOW ONE

4. Britain spends £450 million on them every Christmas. What?
a) Mince pies
b) Chocolates
c) Presents for favourite teachers

5. They've been on Earth nine million years longer than humans. What?
a) Reindeer
b) Turkeys
c) Santa's Elves

6. Put them end to end and they'd go almost four times round the world. What?
a) The Christmas wrapping paper bought each year.
b) The toilet paper used on Christmas Day.
c) Old men pretending to be Father Christmas in shops.

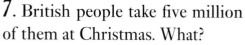

7. British people take five million of them at Christmas. What?
a) Indigestion tablets
b) Baths
c) Seats in church

8. Put them end to end and they'd stretch to the moon. What?
a) The rolls of sticky tape we buy for Christmas.
b) The Christmas puddings we buy each Christmas.
c) Christmas dinner Brussels sprouts.

Answers:

1b) Half a billion pounds worth of £20 notes would stretch 2,188 miles – if they didn't blow away, of course.

2b) Christmas Day and Boxing Day lunches add an average 2 or 3 kilos to each person making a total of 158,000 tonnes. As for the tinsel, one small factory makes over 24,000 miles of the stuff. Enough to go to Australia and back.

3a) That's 140 million on the busiest days. Imagine the size of the postman's sack needed to carry that lot!

4b) Enjoy your Christmas chocolate and don't worry – there are millions of pounds worth of mince pies to eat too.

5b) Of course you can tell if you're unlucky enough to get a 10-million-year-old turkey because it will be a bit tough.

6a) A cheap way to give your loved one the world – wrapped. That wrapping paper costs just £155 million.

7a) That's just one popular make of indigestion tablet. Some people may even take the tablets in the bath!

8a) That's over 240,000 miles … as you probably know. But who went to the moon with a tape measure to check the distance?

FOUL FOOD

People like to pig out at Christmas on festive food. But you can spoil their appetites by telling them what people used to eat in the past!

Stuffed turkeys

A lot of turkeys are bred in Norfolk. But Norfolk is a long way from many of the large cities of Britain where they are eaten. The question is, how would you get a turkey from Norfolk to London in the early 1800s? There were no good railways … and anyway the turkeys couldn't afford the tickets. There were no bicycles or cars or buses. So how did the turkeys get to London?

They *walked*! It was about 100 miles and it took a week.

Imagine that! Not only are you going to have your neck twisted – you have to wear your little legs out before you get the pleasure.

The big birds' feet aren't made for this sort of turkey-trot. Farmers had to make boots out of sacking or leather for the turkeys.

Geese were just as badly off and faced long walks to market at Christmas. But geese didn't like wearing sack shoes so their feet were dipped in soft tar that went hard.

NOT FAIR! YOU GET SLINKY LITTLE LEATHER SLIP-ONS AND I GET STICKY BLACK GOO

Victoria's stuffing

When the turkeys got to London then one lucky bird would be selected for Queen Victoria's own dinner. She had the turkey roasted in a rich pastry. But the stuffing was a bit unusual. Three other birds were killed and their bones removed:

A woodcock was placed inside … a pheasant … which was put inside … a chicken … which was put inside … the turkey.

When it was carved the meat had the different flavours of the four birds.

OO, YUMMY! WOOPHICKEY!

Plucked peacock

People have always enjoyed big birds for Christmas dinner. But turkeys were only discovered by Europeans after Chris Columbus found America in 1492. (The daft birds just stood there and let the Spanish sailors brain them with clubs.)

So before turkeys the Christmas cooks had to use peacocks and swans. But they really knew how to party in the Middle Ages. The birds weren't just roasted and stuck on a plate. No! They were works of art! Want to liven up your Christmas dinner table this year? Here's how …

- Kill your peacock carefully so you don't damage its feathers – a twist of the neck is better than a chainsaw.
- Using a sharp knife (ask an adult to do this for you, kids) remove the skin and feathers in one piece.
- Stick your hand up the peacock's bum and pull its insides out – feed them to the cat or use them to make gravy or parcel them in nice wrapping paper and send them to someone you hate.
- Roast the peacock till it's done.
- Stick the roast peacock inside the peacock's skin and feathers (a twisted coat-hanger may help keep the neck upright) and place it on a large dish. Play pass the peacock before the meal so everyone can admire the cook's craft.

Q. HAVE YOU HEARD ABOUT THE STUPID TURKEY?
A. IT WAS LOOKING FORWARD TO CHRISTMAS!

Umble pie

Here's a jolly Christmas treat for a peasant like you! At Christmas dinner the lords and ladies ate juicy steaks from the dear little deer they'd hunted to death. But it was a shame to waste what was left of butchered Bambi. The servants got the deer 'umbles'.

Cookery Course for Coarse Cooks
Umble pie

Ingredients:
Chopped deer umbles – the heart, liver, tongue, feet, ears and brains
Chopped beef, oysters, bacon and rabbit
Dried fruit
Pastry

To cook:
Stew the umbles and the other meat till tender, then place in a pie dish.
Cover the stewed umbles with the dried fruit and a crust.
Bake till the crust is crisp and brown.

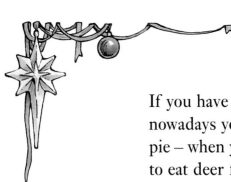

If you have come down in the world and have to do as you are told then nowadays you are said to 'eat humble pie'. In fact that should be 'umble' pie – when you are forced to eat deer feet and brain mash with the peasants.

THE COOK HAD A STUMBLE AND JUMBLED CRUMBLE IN YOUR UMBLE

Boar's head

Here's another pagan custom, popular in Britain and Scandinavia till the 1600s.

Catch and kill a wild boar, cut off its head and roast it as an offering to the goddess of farming. Do this at Christmas and she'll make sure you have a good harvest the following year.

One of the earliest Christmas carols printed in English is the Boar's Head Carol. It is in a 1521 book by Wynkyn de Worde (no I did *not* make up his daft name). This carol was written after a curious battle between a boar and a student of Queen's College, Oxford.

One day a student was walking in Shotover forest with his nose buried in a very interesting book. Suddenly a wild boar rushed out and attacked him.

The student had no time to draw his sword, so he rammed his book down the boar's mouth and it choked to death. He then cut off the head and carried it back to the college in triumph.

At Queen's College, Oxford, the boar's head ceremony still goes on in memory of this monster-mashing deed. The head is now made of jellied meats pressed into a mould and it is carried in by three bearers. Ahead of it walk trumpeters and the choir, who sing the Boar's Head Carol.

Does that make your dinner look feeble? Did your dad's cabbages look

crinkly this year? Were Mum's potatoes pathetic? Then simply sacrifice a boar! Of course they're extinct in Britain. Why? Because so many people chopped their heads off for a Christmas custom!

☠☠ HORRIBLE HISTORIES WARNING ☠☠

Do NOT sacrifice a history teacher's head at Christmas! History teachers are bores but they are not boars.

Paint that pig

After a boar's head had been boiled and stuffed, it looked too pale so the cooks darkened the skin so it looked like a real boar. What did they have in their greasy, smoky kitchens to rub into the skin to darken it?

a) Ink
b) Soot
c) Black pepper

Answer:
b) They mixed pig grease with soot and smeared it on. Yeuch!

Twelfth Night cake

Twelfth Night (6 January) is the end of Christmas when all the decorations come down – or you'll have bad luck. It used to be time for the best party of the year. A special cake was baked with a bean in it. If you got the bean then you were King or Queen of the Bean – everyone had to do as you told them!

The bad news was there were other things baked in the cake:

- If you got a clove you were a villain.
- If you got a twig you were a fool.
- If you got a rag you were a tarty girl.

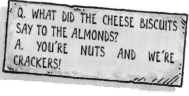

Q. WHAT DID THE CHEESE BISCUITS SAY TO THE ALMONDS?
A. YOU'RE NUTS AND WE'RE CRACKERS!

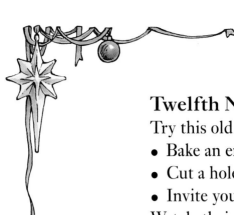

Twelfth Night pie

Try this old Twelfth Night pie joke.

- Bake an empty pie case.
- Cut a hole in the bottom and fill the case with live birds.
- Invite your friends to cut a slice.

Watch their faces as the birds fly out – unless the cutting knife goes through one of the birds, of course. No prizes for guessing this is where the nursery rhyme 'Four and twenty blackbirds' came from.

They teach you at infant school that 'When the pie was opened the birds began to sing'. What teacher never tells you is that the pie wasn't always filled with birds – anything could be inside. A popular jolly Twelfth Night joke was to fill the pie with frogs. Try that and watch your friends hop it!

The truth about Jack's plum

Little Jack Horner
Sat in the corner,
Eating a Christmas pie;
He put in his thumb,
And pulled out a plum,
And said, What a good boy am I!

What is the truth behind that old nursery rhyme? In fact it's a Christmas story.

Jack Horner was a monk who worked for the Abbot of Glastonbury Abbey. 'King Henry VIII will pull down the abbey!' the Abbot moaned. 'What can we do to stop him?'

Jack scratched the bald patch the monks have on top of their head. 'Why don't we just give him the lands. We'll stay here and care for the lands. At least we won't be thrown out!'

30

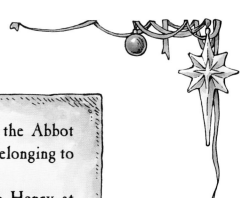

'Brilliant, Horner! Good chap! Always said you were!' the Abbot nodded. 'The deeds are in my desk. There are twelve farms belonging to the abbey. I'll give them all!'

Jolly Jack had another bright idea. 'If I take them to Henry at Hampton it'll be Christmas before I get there. Why don't we present them as a Christmas present?'

'What sort of present?'

'Bake them into a Christmas pie!'

'Brilliant, Horner!' the Abbot agreed and ordered the crust to be baked.

Jack Horner set off with the deeds to the twelve farms and presented Henry VIII with a pie. The King opened the pie and pulled out eleven deeds. He was a happy chappie.

But what had happened to the twelfth deed? Surely Jack Horner hadn't sat in some dark corner and pulled out the deeds to the best farm of all! The 'plum' land?

Oh yes he had!

And that's (supposed to be) the true story behind the nursery rhyme. Now you know.

Mince pies

In the Middle Ages there was always a large mince pie baked for Christmas. But, unlike today's sweet mince, the cooks put all sorts of shredded meat in along with fruit and spices.

The shape of this pie was later changed to make it look like a baby's cradle, or Jesus' crib. By the 1600s cooks were adding a pastry baby Jesus. The Puritans were shocked by this and chief Puritan Oliver Cromwell banned the baked babe.

Of course the British people still wanted their mince pie so they simply made them in the round shape that we eat now. Even when Cromwell died and the Puritans lost their

power in the 1660s the Christmas pies never went back to their crib shape.

By Victorian times the minced meat was left out, but the pies kept the name.

For luck …

Everyone knows you have to leave a mince pie for the fat feller that slides down your chimney each Christmas – if you don't then he may not leave

you any presents. He must get pretty sick of eating millions of mince pies in one night! In the USA they leave him milk and biscuits – and they still get presents!

But do you know the old superstitions about mince pies?

Eat one pie each day on the 12 days leading up to Christmas. This will give you 12 months of luck. But you must eat each pie in a different house. If you haven't 12 friends then you're out of luck – and if you're out of luck then you won't have 12 months' luck so you'll stay out of luck. Tough luck.

Each Christmas, as you take your first bite of your first mince pie, you can make a wish. Don't waste the wish!

For bad luck

Watch out! If you refuse to eat the first mince pie someone offers you then you will suffer bad luck.

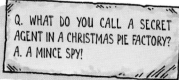

Q. WHAT DO YOU CALL A SECRET AGENT IN A CHRISTMAS PIE FACTORY?
A. A MINCE SPY!

Monster munch

Cooks in the 1700s began to compete to make the richest pie. One nobleman, living in London in 1770, had a pie carried down from the kitchens of his northern castle. Give the recipe to your school dinner cooks! They'll need …

- Four geese, two turkeys, two rabbits, four wild ducks, two woodcocks, six snipe, four partridges, two curlews, seven blackbirds, six pigeons and two ox tongues.
- A pastry case measuring three metres around the outside.

The monster mince munchie weighed over 75 kilos and had to be surrounded with metal bands while it baked to prevent it bursting out of the oven and attacking the cooks.

How could this pie be served at the Christmas table? It was fitted with wheels!

Christmas dinner delights

Each country has its own Christmas favourite food. For some reason in Peru it is a heart of a bull, steeped in spices and wine-vinegar then roasted over an open fire.

That may not be to your taste. But look at Paris, Christmas 1870.

The Prussian army was outside the city stopping any food from getting in. The posh restaurant 'Voisins' was not going to be beaten. They would provide a Christmas dinner to remember.

But where do you get meat when your city is under siege?

Three places: the zoo, the streets and the sewers.

That Christmas 'Voisins' served …

~ Menu ~
· Elephant soup
· Roast kangaroo
· Antelope meat paste
· A whole cat decorated with rats

BOING!

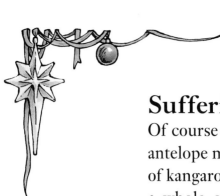

Suffering sprouts

Of course some kids would enjoy a trunk full of elephant soup. To them antelope meat paste would be good gnus – they would leap at the chance of kangaroo meat. They would whisker roasted rat down their gullets and a whole cat would be purrfect. But those kids would *never* touch a Brussels sprout.

Brussels sprouts are first mentioned in books in 1587 and children have suffered them as a Christmas 'treat' ever since.

Want an excuse to avoid the veg that tastes of a tramp's shoe? Then blind your parent with science. Which of these foul food facts is true? Turn to your parent and say, 'Sorry, dear parent, I'd love to eat that smashing sprout but I can't because I've discovered …'

a) … it's been scientifically proven that the bodies of young people cannot cope with the green chemical in sprouts. A child who eats too many sprouts will turn green and look a bit like a lost Martian (fig I).

b) … the chemicals in sprouts react with the bacteria in the stomach to produce hydrogen sulphide. This of course is the gas that is used to make stink bombs. Someone making this gas in their stomach will have to expel the stinking gas through their bottoms and perfume the room with the smell of rotten eggs (fig II).

c) … sprouts taste bitter because the vegetable uses that taste as a chemical weapon. Any insects eating the sprout would be sick … and so will I! (fig III).

d) … children have different taste-buds to adults and they find Brussels sprouts much more bitter than a wrinklie like you would (fig IV).

Answer:
b), c) AND d) are all true. Try them all! Sadly your parents may say, 'Eating sprouts will do you good.' The awful truth is they are right!

 # SAVAGE STORIES

SITTING ROUND THE FIRE, TELLING GHOST STORIES, I'VE FOUND A LEGEND FROM THE NORTH OF ENGLAND. VERY NASTY, BUT IT'S SAID TO BE TRUE!

The Sedgefield spook

It was Christmas Day 1792 in Sedgefield and all the poor people headed for the local rectory. They dragged their frozen feet over furrowed fields to pay their rent to the church rector.

Tom limped along with his father and whined the way kids do. 'Da! How much further?'

'Shut up and mind you don't drop me!' his father, Farmer Fitchett, growled.

Tom steadied the wheelbarrow and went on to the great gateway of the rectory. When they reached the steps he gently lowered his father into a group of grumbling farmers. Seth Sumpbottom turned out his empty pockets. 'He's taken my last penny! It'll be cold Christmas gruel for my family today!'

'Arrrr! That be right that be!' the other farmers agreed.

Farmer Fitchett shook his head till the lice dropped on to the cold steps. 'Best get it over with,' he sighed. He stepped into the dark hallway. 'The rector's too mean to spend a penny on a candle to light our way,' he grumbled to Tom who limped behind him.

 LISTEN TO 'THE SEDGEFIELD SPOOK' ON YOUR FREE CD!

They groped their way along the passage and reached a dark oak door at the end. Fitchett knocked. 'Come in!' a woman's voice cried.

Tom narrowed his eyes, expecting to be dazzled by the light glinting on the piles of gold and silver, the way it always did. But, when the door opened, there was just blackness in the room … blackness and a horrible smell.

'Farmer Fitchett?' the woman asked.

'Arrrr! Ma'am!' Tom's father mumbled.

A little light spilled through the closed curtains. The boy could just make out the needle-nosed woman. Next to her in the gloomy room sat the silent and still rector. 'Good morning, Rector!' Tom said brightly. 'Mother says you've been ill. I hope you're feeling better!' Then the boy coughed as the sharp smell stung his nose and made his eyes water.

The rector didn't reply.

The woman spoke sharply. 'The rector is sick. But not too sick to take your money! That'll be forty guineas, Fitchett,' she said.

The farmer threw a bag of coins on the table. The rector's wife snatched the bag, spilled the coins and counted quickly. 'Good day, Farmer Fitchett. Close the door when you leave.'

Tom and his father backed towards the door. The boy gasped at the musty air of the corridor. 'Penniless, boy, we're penniless till next market day,' his father moaned. 'I wish that illness had killed the old rector,' he snarled.

'Why, father?' Tom asked.

'Because if the rector died before Christmas Day we would not have to pay that forty guineas! We'd have plum pudding and fresh duck for dinner this day! Now, wheel me home, son.'

'I wheeled you here.' Tom said softly.

'Well that means it's your turn to wheel me back!'

Next day, Boxing Day, the news was all around the village of Sedgefield. 'The rector is dead!' they said. 'A day too late!' they groaned.

That night, as the farmers sat drinking in the tavern on the village green, a grim and grey-faced doctor walked in. 'Is he dead?' a sour-faced Farmer Fitchett asked.

The doctor nodded. 'Dead at least two weeks, I'd say!'

'Two weeks! But I saw him yesterday, Christmas Day! We all did!' the farmer cried and Seth joined him with a puzzled, 'Arrrr!'

'The rector's wife wanted your rent,' the doctor said. 'She had to pretend he was alive until she got it.'

'She couldn't keep a mouldy body two whole weeks!' the inn-keeper's wife said (though most of her pigeon pies were twice as old as that).

'That's why she soaked him in pickle vinegar,' the doctor explained.

'That was the smell! The nasty smell!' Tom cried, spilling his ale in his excitement.

'Let's go get our money back!' Farmer Fitchett bellowed louder than his old bull.

'Arrrr!' his farm friends cried. The doctor tried to tell them that the rector's wife had left on the six o'clock stagecoach to York, but they didn't listen. They ran over to the rectory. Farmer Fitchett didn't even wait for his wheelbarrow. The sky glowed orange and red ahead of them. The villagers stopped and stared up at the burning building.

Most of the rectory was swallowed by the fierce flame. One tower window was still dark. As the frightened folk looked up a greenly-glowing face looked down on them. 'The parson! The pickled parson's pickled ghost!' a woman screamed. Suddenly flames burst through the tower and it collapsed into the shattered shell of the house.

Since that day the grisly, greenly-glowing ghost has never been seen again. But ask the people of Sedgefield if the story is true and it's for sure they'll say, 'Arrrr!'

Rotten rent collectors

Christmas is a 'quarter day' – no, that doesn't mean it's six hours long. It means it's a day when rents were paid to the landowners and landlords. (That's why the peasants of Sedgefield went to their rectory on Christmas Day.)

There's another shocking (but true) story from the north of England. It happened in Well, near Richmond, in North Yorkshire in 1289.

The local parson expected a visit from the king's rent collector on Christmas Day that year. The rent collector would expect to stay the night. The trouble is the parson had broken the church rules – he had a girlfriend and the rent collector would report the parson to the king if he saw her living at the rectory. So the parson stuck the young woman in his strongroom.

She looked around the room and it was stuffed with the rent money. Soon it was her dress that was stuffed with money as she slipped a fat purse down the front of it. 'Let me out!' she cried. 'I need a pee!'

When the parson let her out she ran off with the money. Of course the rent collector found that the money was missing. The parson got the blame and the sack.

ROTTEN CHRISTMAS

Christmas is a time of happiness and joy – that's what they say, but some people have had a horrible Christmas in the past. Christmas has been as cruel as any other day really. Just look at the last century …

1917 In Canada the ship *Mont Blanc* is full of explosives when she is rammed by another ship, killing 1,635 people on 6 December.

1924 Christmas Eve and Britain's worst air disaster to date. An airliner crashes soon after take-off in London and manages to hit a housing estate. Eight people die. On Christmas Day 1952 an aeroplane will crash at Prestwick airport and then 28 will die. Bigger aeroplanes mean more are killed. That's progress.

1930 Kids are crammed in to see a pantomime at the Iroquois Theatre, Chicago. When fire breaks out 200 die from the smoke and another 400 are trampled to death in the crush to escape.

1932 In Glasgow, jobless people have a protest march, and 15 are injured when they clash with police. The marchers react with an ancient Glasgow custom and throw a policeman into the freezing Clyde river.

1940 German aircraft bomb Manchester with some highly explosive crackers. One thousand and five people killed, which rather spoils their Christmas.

1952 Four thousand Londoners die of breathing problems caused by 'smog' (smoky fog) over the Christmas period. The smoke from the jolly Christmas coal fires has caused it.

1953 Volcano Ruapehu erupts in New Zealand and its lava blocks the river Whangaehu which bursts its banks and flattens a railway bridge which the Wellington to Auckland express is crossing – 150 victims.

1972 The capital city of Nicaragua, Managua, is destroyed by an earthquake.

1974 A cyclone called Tracy hits Australia's Northern Territory on Christmas Day – or was it just Santa's sleigh swishing through? Houses torn up, boats and planes and trains wrecked. $250 million bill for this Christmas present.

1989 The President of Romania and his wife have been arrested. Today they are tied down on Christmas chairs and executed with Christmas bullets.

1999 Usual Merry Christmas. Warnings of terrorist bombs in the mail for Brits and Americans; an Indian airliner is hijacked and a passenger shot; Russian troops use tanks and planes to flatten women and children in Chechnya; storms in southern Britain flood homes and drown people.

2004 Thirty families are thrown out of their homes in Milwaukee (USA) because the mould in their flats is giving off a poison gas … JUST like the first Christmas! No proper home and those oxen and asses giving off poison gases! Nothing much has changed in 200 years then.

On Boxing Day a Tsunami hits Asia and kills over 200,000 people.

Christmas crime

Christmas is prime crime time. Of course crooks have to watch out for the fir tree police – they're from special branch!

1 Stone stealers. In 1950 Scottish nationalists sneak into Westminster Abbey in London. What do they pinch? A lump of stone. But a very special 152kg lump of stone known as the Stone of Scone. Scottish kings had been crowned on this stone till Edward I of England nicked it.

2 Un-fair competition. In Berlin in the 1990s Christmas tree sellers went to war. One seller advertized £25 trees for just £6 and the other

sellers almost went out of business. They threatened to kill their rival and he had to hire bodyguards. Christmas fairs there are just as vicious – the brakes on the rides are loosened and the light bulbs are fused so the owners have to close down or spend a lot of money on repairs.

3 Fir coated. People pinch Christmas trees. Instead of buying them from tree farmers some people walk into a fir wood and hack down a tree. But trees cost money to grow – firs just don't grow on trees … if you see what I mean. In the north of England, Durham Council became fed up with tree thieves in their plantations. Guard dogs cost too much, and probably would have used the trees for pees! So how did they stop tree thieves? They sprayed the trees with something disgusting that wouldn't harm the tree. What did they choose? Human poo from a nearby sewage plant. Yeuch!

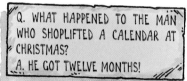

Q. WHAT HAPPENED TO THE MAN WHO SHOPLIFTED A CALENDAR AT CHRISTMAS?
A. HE GOT TWELVE MONTHS!

CHRISTMAS BORED GAME

For this game you'll need dice and counters. If you've lost your dice under the sofa, you could mark a six-sided pencil with one to six dots and roll that instead, and you could use pennies as counters. Take turns rolling the dice and move on the number of spaces shown. If you land on a question you can give yourself a mince pie for a right answer and a liver-and-kidney pie for a wrong one. (You'll find the answers on page 98.)

The first to the end gets the prize of a snowball up the nose. The loser gets a snowball down the back.

Ready? Here we go.

START

1 Who was Scrooge's first ghostly visitor?
a) Jacob Marley
b) Christmas Past

2 What do Dutch children hang up for presents?
a) stockings
b) shoes

3 Bonus
You succeed in sprinkling holly prickles in your history teacher's toilet roll. Go forward two spaces – quickly!

4 Penalty
You eat too much Christmas pudding and vomit on the cat. Go back two places to mop it up.

5 Santa has a reindeer called ...
a) Blitzen
b) Bambi

6 Australians celebrate Christmas by ...
a) sledging
b) surfing

7 In Finland Santa's sleigh is pulled by ...
a) a goat called Ukko
b) a duck called Dukko

8 Penalty
Your hamster escapes and chews through the Christmas lights cable and electrocutes itself. Miss a turn while you hold a funeral.

9 Bonus
The Christmas fairy grants you three wishes. You leap ahead three places.

10 Poet Dylan Thomas wrote 'A Child's Christmas in ...'
a) Wales
b) Lapland

11 Bonus
You find reindeer droppings on your roof. You post it through the letterbox of your nasty neighbour. Run for your life two spaces.

12 Penalty
The Christmas fairy turns out to be a dream. Go back three places and roll the dice again.

13 In the poem 'The Night before Christmas' nothing was stirring, not even a ...
a) moose
b) mouse

14 The world's largest cracker (50 metres long) was made in 1991 in ...
a) Australia
b) Austria

15 In 1975 Werner Ehrhard sent a record number of Christmas cards, a total of ...
a) 2,824
b) 62,824

16 Penalty
You are overjoyed to see snow on Christmas Eve. While sledging you catch pneumonia and spend Christmas Day in hospital. Miss two turns.

17 Bonus
Your family turn vegetarian on Christmas Eve and your pet turkey (called Trotsky) is saved. Roll again!

18
In Old England people drank a hot ale and apple brew at Christmas called …
a) dogs-breath
b) lambs-wool

19 Penalty
Your family numbers win the Christmas lottery, but the cat ate the ticket. Go back to square one.

20
Before pantomimes Christmas plays were performed by …
a) mummers
b) mummies

21
Which of these is NOT one of Santa's reindeer?
a) Blitzen
b) Klaxon

22 Penalty
The Bang of your cracker scares the cat up the curtains – miss a turn.

23 Bonus
You offer your favourite teacher mistletoe and she eats it. Move forward two places as you speed to hospital.

24
In the Ukraine you find a spider in the house. This means …
a) your house needs cleaning
b) good luck

25
You find a button in your Christmas pudding. What does that mean?
a) You'll be rich
b) You won't get married

26 Penalty
You try to throw a bucket of water over carol singers but the water turns to a block of ice and you crack a singing skull. Go back two spaces to hide.

27
You are given frumenty at a Christmas party. Do you …
a) eat it
b) give it to the cat

28
Which of these two was one of the wise men?
a) Caspar
b) Gasper

29
Who wrote *The Father Christmas Letters*?
a) Father Christmas of course you dummy
b) J R R Tolkien (who wrote *The Hobbit* and *Lord of the Rings*)

30 Penalty
A giant snowball rolls over you and sweeps you down the hill to where you started. Return to square one.

FINISH

SILLY SANTA

WHAT DO YOU CALL A FAT, UNSHAVEN OLD MAN WHO TRIMS HIS RED SUIT WITH THE FUR OF MURDERED ERMINE? SAINT NICHOLAS, SANTA CLAUS OR FATHER CHRISTMAS

Here are some things they never tell you about Santa.

1 The real Saint Nicholas was a rich bishop who lived in Myra (which is now part of Turkey) in the fourth century. It's said that he felt pity on a father and three daughters who were very poor. What did Saint Nick do? He walked past the windows of the girls and lobbed in bags of gold! There may even be some truth in that story – some say he dropped it down the chimney, where it fell into the shoe or stocking she had left on the hearth to keep warm. And that's why children hang up their stocking or leave a shoe ready for presents! You can see why he became a saint of giving presents, but his feast day is really 6 December.

2 Old pictures of Saint Nicholas showed him surrounded by three purses of gold. But the pictures were badly painted and the purses were mistaken for children's heads! A story grew that the children had been murdered by an innkeeper and pickled in salt water. (Don't ask me why!) Along came Saint Nick who brought them back to life. Definitely untrue, but Saint Nicholas became a saint of children.

3 French priests of the 1950s claimed Santa was not a Christian figure … so he must be a creature of the devil. (Makes sense.) They built a bonfire and burned a Santa figure on it. In 1969 the Pope agreed that Saint Nicholas was not such a great saint, but the fact is he'd become more popular than ever.

4 Santa's visit hasn't always been a fun and exciting thing. In Holland it could be pretty scary. The problem was the Dutch Santa Claus (called Sinter Klaas by Dutch children who are clearly rotten at spelling) had a little friend with him called Black Peter. Unpopular Pete carried a whip with him and it was his job to flog children who'd been naughty! Sinter Klaas goes around on 5 December – which is probably a good idea. It

means he can miss out Holland on his busiest night. When the Dutch in the USA took Sinter across the Atlantic they dropped poor Black Peter (probably in the ocean).

5 How do we know Santa has a red suit, a white beard and black boots when no one has seen him because he travels too fast? In 1931 the Coca Cola drink company wanted a picture of Santa for their Christmas advert. The American artist Haddon Sundblom created the idea of red-suited Santa. Maybe Haddon met Santa … or maybe he made it all up. Maybe Santa looks completely different! Maybe she's a skinny woman in a blue boiler suit. We'll never know.

6 In 1999 three hundred Santas went on strike in Berlin. The Santas had always been paid for their part-time work – around £20 every time they visited someone's house with presents; on Christmas Eve they could make £250. But the government decided to make the Santas pay tax, so their £250 became less than £200.

Q. WHAT DOES SANTA USE TO WEED HIS GARDEN?
A. A HOE–HOE–HOE!

7 Soldiers decided that it was good to have Santa on your side in battles. In the American Civil War of the 1860s he was pictured wearing the Yankee Stars and Stripes flag instead of his usual robes. In the Afghan wars of the 1870s he was shown as a British soldier charging at the Afghans with a rifle. What happened to peace and goodwill to all men at Christmas? The words 'Peace and Goodwill' were written in the snow and Santa was trampling over them – the message was clear, peace and goodwill to all men … except the enemy!

8 Germans in the 1600s decided that the Christ Child should be worshipped at Christmas. They called him Christkindl – German for Christ Child. This name changed to Kriss Kringle and became a name for Santa Claus. So the Germans tried to make Christmas about Christ but failed.

9 American shops have so many visitors to see Santa in the grotto they have to have a dozen or more fellers to dress up as Santa. Some of the Santas have been grotty in the grotto and shop managers have had to make rules for the foul Father Christmas fakers. Here are some of them:

Santa Rules

- Make sure you wear clean socks and underpants so you don't smell.
- Don't eat garlic or chew tobacco so your breath smells sweet.
- Don't hit the children or their parents no matter how nasty they may get.
- Have clean fingernails and trim the hair in your nose.
- In an emergency (like a child being sick on Santa) send for a replacement Santa at once.
- No swearing, drinking or taking tips from the parents.

10 Italian presents were once delivered by an old woman, La Befana. The story was that the Three Wise Men had stopped at Befana's house to invite her to visit the Christ Child. Befana had lost her child in a plague and was too upset to think about visiting another baby. Then the daft bat changed her mind, jumped on her broomstick and flew after the Wise Men. She never found them, but every time she came across a good child's stocking she filled it with toys and sweets. But bad news for you wicked kids … when she came across a bad child she filled their stocking with coal. (At least you won't freeze!)

Silly Santa story

Father Christmas landed on the roof of a house and squashed the family cat that was up there. Santa knocked on the door and said to the mother of the family, 'I'm sorry, I've squidged your cat. Can I replace it?'

The woman thought about it and said, 'I don't know … are you any good at catching mice?'

Hot reindeer

Scientists have worked out how Santa Claus could deliver all those presents in one night:

- 842 million houses
- almost 2,000 million kilos of toys
- travelling 220 million miles

The bad news is his huge sleigh (needing 214,200 reindeer to pull it) would behave like a meteorite.

Have you heard of meteorites? Lumps of rock that fall to earth so quickly they burn up with a flash in the sky? Well Santa's reindeer (all 214,200 of them) would burn up just like that. How long would they last? About 1/250th of a second. They'd be gone with a sizzle and the scent of burned reindeer meat.

The only way Santa could do the trip would be for him to be a time traveller. No one has invented a time machine … yet. But if Santa invents one in the future then he can travel back to make sure you get your presents next Christmas!

Santa's four-legged helper

Rudolf is not an ancient tale of a darling deer. He was created for an advert in 1939.

Robert May worked in the advertising section of the Montgomery Ward department store in Chicago. He came up with an idea for a new kind of Christmas gift for children – a poem about one of Santa's deer with a bright red nose who helped his master find his way from chimney to chimney.

Of course the poor little deer was bullied and picked on by the other reindeer because of his crimson conk. If you had a shiny snotter you'd be picked on too! What's the answer to the bullying? Tell the teacher? Fight back and beat up the bullies? No! Wait for a foggy night and lead everyone safely home! Just think about it … how does a red nose help you find your way in the fog? Your nose would have to be like a floodlight! Where would a reindeer keep its batteries?

In that first Christmas, every child who visited the store's resident Santa received a booklet of 'Rudolph the Red-Nosed Reindeer'. More than 2.4 million copies were given away free.

In 1949 Johnny Marks, a friend of Robert May, decided to set the poem to music. He approached various singers to record it, without success. Finally, Gene Autry, a singing cowboy, agreed to record it. The record zoomed to the top of the hit parade. Next to Bing Crosby's 'White Christmas', Autry's version of 'Rudolph the Red-Nosed Reindeer' is one of the biggest-selling records of all time! Since it was first released, there have been over 300 versions of the song, and more than 80 million records sold.

Anyway, Rudolf the reindeer almost had a different name. Robert May came up with two names that the shop managers turned down. Can your parents tell you what *two* names Rudolf almost had from the following five?

a) Rollo
b) Rambo
c) Rumpo
d) Reginald
e) Ringo

Answer:

a) and **d)** Ask yourself, would 'Reginald the Red-Nosed Reindeer' have done as well?

Q. WHY DOES SANTA GO DOWN SMOKE-BLACK CHIMNEYS?
A. BECAUSE IT SOOTS HIM!

The chimney

Why does Father Christmas go to all the trouble of squeezing down chimneys when he could just dump your presents on the doorstep, knock on the door and zoom off on his sleigh?

a) Because Saint Nicholas was the saint of chimney sweeps.

b) Because there was a pagan legend about a goddess who arrived down the chimney.

c) Because doors hadn't been invented when he first started visting houses and now he's used to dropping in.

Answer:

b) It may be to do with German pagan goddess Hertha. During the winter festival each house would be decorated with fir boughs and other evergreens to welcome her. A platform of stones, like an altar, was built in the hearth – a word that comes from her name. Evergreens were burned on this platform. Hertha would follow the smoke signals, come down through the smoke of the blazing branches, and reward the good. The bad news is she would also have the job of punishing the bad.

CHRISTMAS CHARACTERS

Saint Stephen

Saint Stephen's Day is 26 December – Boxing Day it's called now. Saint Stephen was the first person to die for preaching about Jesus. His enemies stood him against a wall and pelted him with stones till he was pulped to death. It's no surprise he became the saint of headaches!

There is a nasty legend that Saint Stephen was about to escape from prison, while his jailers were asleep, but chirruping wrens woke up the guards and Stephen was caught. As a result there was a charming Irish custom of punishing wrens on Saint Stephen's Day by stoning the little chirpers to death.

The boys who killed a wren would tie it to a pole and go from house to house begging. They'd offer a wren's feather for luck in exchange for money. If there's one thing worse than being a dead wren it's being a dead bald wren. This custom was still being carried out in the 1920s.

Saint Anastasia

Now you may think that Christmas Day is Saint Nicholas's Day because, of course, Saint Nick is Santa Claus. But 25 December is actually Saint Anastasia's day. Young Anastasia was the wife of a pagan Roman. She started looking after Christians in prison so ended up in prison herself. Don't worry! The dead Saint Theodota kept Anastasia supplied with food (a neat trick if you can manage it). Anastasia was then put on a ship and it was left to drift till it sank. But don't worry! Dead Saint Theodota guided the ship to land! Finally Anastasia had her arms and legs tied to stakes in the ground. A pile of wood was built over her and set alight. (Dead Saint Theodota mustn't have been handy with a fire extinguisher.)

Saint Boniface

It didn't do to mess with Boniface. He was one tough medieval English monk.

One day he came across a bunch of pagans in northern Europe, gathered around an oak tree. 'Here!' Boniface boomed. 'What do you think you're doing with that child?'

The pagan sneered at the massive monk. 'What's it to you? As it happens we are going to sacrifice the child to the great god Thor at this sacred oak tree! Cut his throat and scatter the blood on the roots!'

'Oh no you're not!' Boniface breathed.

The pagan would have replied, 'Oh yes we are!' but pantomimes hadn't been invented. Instead he said, 'Who's going to stop us?'

Boniface bulged his biceps and swung his fist at the tree. It was knocked clean out of the ground. In its place a fir tree began to grow.

'Phwoar!' the pagans panted and fell to their nasty knees.

Boniface explained, 'This is a tree that doesn't lose its leaves in winter, so it's the tree of everlasting life! And our Jesus will offer you everlasting life if you give up your pagan passions and change to our church!'

The pagans were converted, the child was saved … and the Christmas tree has been a Christian sign ever since.

Martin Luther

There's another story about the first Christmas tree. The German preacher, Martin Luther, was walking through the forest one night in the

1520s and admired the stars twinkling through the branches of the fir trees. He cut down a small tree and took it home to show his family how wonderful God's universe is. Of course the kids said, 'But we can't see the stars 'cos we're in the house, Dad!'

So marvellous Martin filled the tree with candles. 'Can you see them now?' he asked.

'Cor, Dad! Can we have one of these every Christmas?' they begged. And so the idea of a

Christmas tree at Christmas was born. (Which is a bit of a cheat when you think about it … they're NOT stars.)

The idea of a fir tree for Christmas spread from Germany to Britain, Scandinavia and North America by the early 1900s – they were all Protestant Christian countries. The countries in southern Europe were Catholic Christians who said at first, 'All that tree worship is shocking! You won't catch us with a filthy fir, friend!'

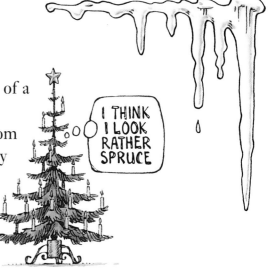

Foul fact

Those old candle-lit Christmas trees may look very pretty on Christmas cards. But what the Christmas cards don't give you is the smell! Most people couldn't afford fine beeswax candles so they used 'tallow' which is usually made from sheep fat. So a room with a Christmas tree would stink of burning sheep fat!

Saint Stephen of Sweden

Saint Stephen of Sweden loved horses. He had five of his own: two chestnut, two white and one dappled. By riding each in turn, Stephen was able to travel great distances on his missionary journeys.

One day, while riding through a lonely forest, he was murdered by a band of men who pinched his valuable horses.

The crafty crooks tied his body on to the back of a wild colt. 'That horse will gallop until it drops,' cried the men, 'and no one will ever find the body!'

By a holy Christmas miracle the horse did not bolt into the wilderness, but carried Stephen gently back to his home at Norrtalje. Of course the men were caught and executed horribly. Stephen's grave became a holy place for horses.

If your horse is sick then take it to Norrtalje. But even better – don't let your horses get sick! Give them a dose of the old bleeding treatment.

Boxing Day is the day for 'bleeding' your horses. Ride your horse till it is sweating then make a cut on its leg to let some blood out. By doing this on Boxing Day you will also let out the evil spirits in your horse.

Saint Thomas

Saint Thomas was made the patron saint of old people and children. In days gone by, old and young were allowed to go round collecting money on 21 December, which is Saint Thomas's Day, to buy food for their Christmas dinners. This custom was called a-Thomasing, or else a-mumping or a-gooding!

The children would give a sprig of holly or mistletoe to anyone who put money in their collecting box. Saint Thomas's Day was often a school holiday, but if they did have to go to school, children made it a day for tricks against the teacher. Sometimes they would lock him out of school and get up to all kinds of fun and games inside on their own.

Charles Dickens

Amazing as it may seem, by the early part of the 1800s Christmas had almost died out. *The Times* newspaper, for example, did not once mention Christmas between 1790 and 1835! People thought it was a silly old-fashioned custom and didn't want to be bothered with it.

Charles Dickens, with his story *A Christmas Carol*, did more than anyone to change all that. The tale of Scrooge, the Cratchits and Tiny Tim has been a smash hit from Victorian times to the present day.

Here's a quick Christmas quiz for those clever people who think they know about books …

1 How long did it take Charles Dickens to write A Christmas Carol?
a) 22 years
b) 2 years
c) 2 months

2 How long did it take for the book to be a hit?
a) It was slow at first but sold out in 10 years.
b) It was an instant success and sold out as soon as it appeared.
c) By the following Christmas (1844) it had sold out.

3 What did Dickens say about his book?
a) 'I was a bit surprised because I've written much better.'
b) 'I'm amazed no one else had the idea. I pinched it from an old Scottish story.'
c) 'The greatest I think I have ever achieved.'

4 Dickens made still more money from the book by doing what?
a) Travelling around the country reading it to the public.
b) Making a record of the story and selling the record.
c) Turning it into a pantomime and acting the part of Scrooge himself.

5 What effect did Dickens's success have on him?
a) All the travelling and performing killed him.
b) It made a jealous writer kill him.
c) It made him so rich his wife killed him to get her hands on his money.

6 When Dickens died it was a shock to the Christmas industry. One little girl said what?
a) 'Does that mean that Father Christmas is dead?'
b) 'Does that mean Tiny Tim is dead?'
c) 'Does that mean there'll be no more Christmases?'

THIS IS A DICKENS OF A NOVEL

HOW THE DICKENS DID HE DO IT?

WHAT A DICKENS DICKENS'S DICKENS IS!

Answers:

1c) He was a very fast writer, and used one of the first fountain pens. He probably wore out quill pens faster than geese could grow the feathers! He began *A Christmas Carol* in early October 1843 and finished at the end of November.

2b) The book was published on 17 December 1843 and immediately sold out. Six thousand copies were sold at five shillings – quite a high price in those days.

3c) Dickens declared that 'the book was a huge success – the greatest I think I have ever achieved!' Well, if you can't praise your own work, who can? Maybe you should learn this line and repeat it to your teacher when you hand in your next piece of writing.

4a) *A Christmas Carol* was so popular that Dickens was asked to read from it in public. His reading from this book (and bits of his longer novels) drew large audiences in England and America, and Dickens made as much money from them as he did from his writing.

5a) The strain that these readings put on him was huge and certainly hastened his death, on 9 June 1870. It was said he 'died of fame'.

6a) Although Charles Dickens had not even mentioned Father Christmas in his story, the little girl's remark shows how important the famous author had become to Christmas.

DAMN THAT DICKENS BUT THANK THE LORD FOR FOUNTAIN PENS

CHRISTMAS ENTERTAINMENT

All those Christmas 'specials' on the telly are nothing new. Christmas has always had 'special' entertainment to keep the people happy.

Mumming and morris madness

Plays for Christmas were first performed in the early Middle Ages with acting groups called 'mummers' and 'morris' dancers.

These men (always men in the Middle Ages) would dress up in masks and dance in the villages for the peasants or in the castles for the posh folk. Some of their costumes were a bit odd. They have been known to dress as a rabbit, a bunch of legs waving in the air (eh?), and a 'Green Man' (dressed like a walking bush). If they were wandering down your High Street today they'd probably get arrested!

I want my mumming

Want to try mumming this Christmas? You can act this in front of the Christmas tree with a few friends on Christmas Day for your parents. The plot is a bit odd and there's a mixture of Pagan and Christian religion in it. All the players black their faces in soot and make whatever costumes they can.

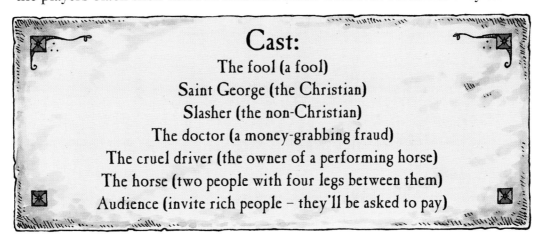

Cast:
The fool (a fool)
Saint George (the Christian)
Slasher (the non-Christian)
The doctor (a money-grabbing fraud)
The cruel driver (the owner of a performing horse)
The horse (two people with four legs between them)
Audience (invite rich people – they'll be asked to pay)

Scene 1:

Fool: Good Christmas to you, friends and neighbours dear!
My, what a handsome crowd we have in here!
(Passes round hat to collect money)

George: In comes I, Saint George, from England did I spring,
My famous name around the world does ring.
Here I draw my bloody weapon.
Show me a man who'll against me stand
I'll cut him down with my brave hand.

Audience: Hooray!

Slasher: I am a valiant soldier, Bold Slasher is my name.
My sword here by my side, I thinks to win the game.
A battle, a battle with George I'll try,
To see which on the ground shall die.

Audience: Boo! Hiss! Get off you nasty man!
(They fight. Saint George is beaten to the ground)

Scene 2:

Fool: Horrible! Terrible! Dead as a Christmas goose!
Is there a doctor to be found,
To cure this man of his deadly wound?
Doctor, doctor! Ten pounds for a doctor!
(Passes round hat to collect money)

Doctor: In comes I that's never come in yet,
The old quack doctor you may bet,
I can cure the magpie of the toothache.
First I tears off his head,
Then I throws his body in the ditch.
And he never has toothache again.
Well, ten pounds is my fee,
But I must take fifteen of thee
Before I set this gallant free!
(Passes round hat to collect money)
Now I have a little bottle in my left-hand waistcoat pocket
called Okum Pokum.

Here George take a little of my nip nap, put it in your snip snack,
Rise up Jack and fight again!
(Saint George arises)

George: Ladies and gentlemen standing round,
See he's cured me safe and sound,
He's healed my wounds and cleansed my blood
And given me something that's done me good.
(Passes round hat to collect money)

Driver: In comes I, the cruel driver,
I'm only ere 'cos this lot promised me a fiver.
(Passes round hat to collect money)
I've got me 'orse tied up outside.
'is famous name's spread far and wide.
He'll dance for you this Christmas Day
If you will just a fiver pay
To buy the good horse lots of hay!
(Horse dances then passes round hat to collect money)

All: Christmas is a-coming and the goose is getting fat,
Please put a penny in the old man's hat.
If you haven't got a penny a ha'penny will do,
If you haven't got a ha'penny, well God bless you.

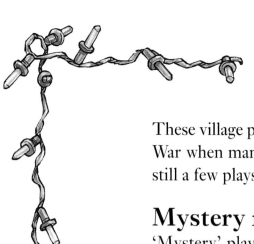

These village plays were passed on from father to son until the First World War when many of the sons were wiped out on the battlefield. There are still a few plays that survive, though no one can agree on the words.

Mystery magic

'Mystery' plays were another type of Christmas entertainment – which had no 'mystery' in them. They were performed by the workmen of the town. (No women again, you'll notice!)

They used to perform the story of Jesus in the churchyard – till the crowds began trampling on the graves and the priests drove them out on to the streets.

The plays were often comedy-horror stories. The comedy came from the simple-minded shepherds – like Hanken, Harvey and Tudde, who spent their time arguing about what exactly the angel of the Lord had said to them. These dim-witted shepherds were kind-hearted folk and they gave their own humble gifts to the infant Jesus. The gifts were:

- a bottle without a stopper
- a cup
- a pair of gloves
- a ball
- an old spoon.

AND YOU THOUGHT YOUR CHRISTMAS PRESENTS WERE FEEBLE! HOW WOULD YOU LIKE THAT LOT?

Herod was a character in mystery plays that everyone loved to hate. Children were terrified, especially when they saw the Massacre of the Innocents.

- Herod would growl, snort, scream, and run around the audience.
- Life-like dummies were used, with lots of pretend blood.
- Herod was dragged down to Hell through a trapdoor out of which real smoke billowed.
- Herod's agonizing screams echoed from under the floorboards of the stage.
- Angels would fly down (attached to wires).

Does this sound like a modern pantomime with goodies to cheer and baddies to hiss?

Panto pleasures

In France in the 1700s spectacular Christmas dances were performed. Jugglers, magicians and acrobats were added and then they began to tell fairy tales – tales like *Babes in the Wood*, *Puss in Boots* or *Sleeping Beauty*. Pantomime had been invented.

Cinderella first appeared in 1860 with Baron Balderdash and his ugly daughters Corinda and Thisbe. The panto had Buttoni – not a type of spaghetti but a character who changed to Buttons.

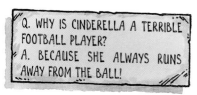

Q. WHY IS CINDERELLA A TERRIBLE FOOTBALL PLAYER?
A. BECAUSE SHE ALWAYS RUNS AWAY FROM THE BALL!

Aladdin appeared in 1881 at a time when ships were trading with China and there was a lot of interest in Chinese things. But where did Aladdin's mother, Widow Twankey get her name? What was a 'twankey'?

a) A Chinese slave who did the washing.

b) A Chinese town where the first Christian missionaries landed and brought Christmas to the country.

c) A type of green tea from China.

Answer:
c) Goodness knows what Chinese pantomime visitors thought of a woman called Widow Green Tea!

Putrid pantos

In Victorian times, instead of actors, comedians were given star parts. They brought in funny songs and terrible jokes that we still have today. 'He's behind you!' and 'Oh, no he isn't!' rang around the Victorian theatres.

One thing that survived from the ancient mumming plays was two people dressed up as a comic horse. The lowest part you could have on stage was the back end of a panto animal. A cheerful little song was written for the actors who proudly played the part. It is a little bit rude … so do NOT read it … especially if there's a nun in the room.

 LISTEN TO 'PUTRID PANTO' ON YOUR FREE CD!

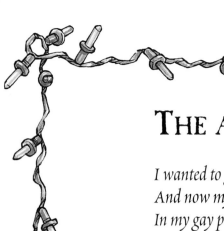

THE ACTOR'S SONG

I wanted to go on the stage,
And now my ambitions I got 'em.
In my gay pantaloons I'm the rage,
As the hole in the elephant's bottom.

My friends all think I'm a wit;
In their seats in the stalls I can spot 'em.
And I wink at the girls in the pit,
Through the hole in the elephant's bottom.

Last night I had some bad luck;
The manager said I was rotten.
I happened to get my head stuck
Through the hole in the elephant's bottom.

My part it is not very large,
Nor yet is it easily forgotten.
If you're looking for me come and look
Through the hole in the elephant's bottom.

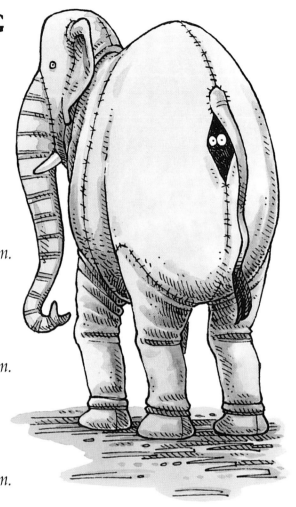

Goose dancing

In the 1750s the young people of the Isles of Scilly went goose dancing at Christmas. But what was goose dancing?

a) Another name for goose butchering – they danced among the geese swinging axes.

b) They danced with geese strapped to their heads which was very tiring. The ones who lasted longest got a prize.

c) It had nothing to do with geese. The men dressed as women and the women dressed as men and they danced.

Answer:
c) The men's dresses were a bit odd, being one colour on the left and another on the right. They went from house to house and danced and were given a drink at each one.

CHRISTMAS CWIZ

OF COURSE KIDS LIKE CHRISTMAS 'COS THERE'S NO SCHOOL, NO TESTS, NO SATS! THAT'S WHY I INVENTED A TEST FOR THEM TO SIT!

You have five minutes to answer 'True' or 'False' to the following facts:

1. The 'X' in Xmas stands for the cross that Jesus died on.
   True☐ False☐

2. In the Middle Ages you could get a ready-cooked goose take away for Christmas.
   True☐ False☐

3. Tinsel is put on Christmas trees because it looks like spiders' webs.
   True☐ False☐

4. Christmas pudding was invented soon after the first Christmas.
   True☐ False☐

5. Rosemary was thrown on the floor at Christmas and trampled by everyone!
   True☐ False☐

6. The popular song 'Jingle Bells' was written specially for Christmas.
   True☐ False☐

7. Santa is dead and buried in Italy.
   True☐ False☐

8. In the USA there is one town called Santa Claus.
   True☐ False☐

9. Tinsel was invented as a Christmas tree decoration.
   True☐ False☐

10. Ducks in Walmer, Kent, get a present every Christmas.
    True☐ False☐

Answers:

1 False. The Greek word for 'Christ' is Xristos and many early Christians spoke Greek. They used 'X' to stand for Christ so X-mas stood for Christ-mas. As years passed and non-Greek Christians forgot the meaning of 'X' they believed 'X' had an old pagan meaning and that to use 'X' for Christ was a sign of disrespect. But it wasn't and it isn't. Now you know!

2 True. The church fixed the price at seven pence – more than a day's wages. You could have a raw goose for six pence. Elizabeth I had goose to celebrate her navy's defeat of the Spanish Armada in 1588. She ordered that English people should have roast goose every Christmas to remember the event. Now you can't even buy a take away goose-burger to celebrate.

3 True. A German story says animals were let into the house at Christmas because Jesus had been born in a stable amongst the animals. But housewives kept spiders out because their webs were messy. (Not as messy as cow-droppings or sheep pee, but they didn't seem to mind that!) Anyway, the spiders were upset and appealed to Jesus for his help. He let them in to see the Christmas trees and they were so excited they spun webs all over them. Jesus turned the webs to tinsel and the housewives were delighted.

HE'S A STAR!

4 False. Long before Christians invented Christmas the pagan Druids told a story of their porridgy fruit pudding – frumenty. Their god of harvests, Dagda, mixed porridge with all the rich foods on earth and gave it to humans for their winter festival.

Pleasant scent

Peasant scent

5 True. Rosemary the herb, that is, not Rosemary the girl! The smell of the crushed leaves gave a pleasant scent and it kept away evil spirits. Legend says that when Mary, Joseph and the baby Jesus fled into Egypt, Mary washed the baby's clothes and spread them out to dry over a rosemary bush, so that they became beautifully scented.

6 False. It was written for the US celebration known as Thanksgiving Day. It was written in 1857 and called 'One horse open sleigh'. The song should not be confused with Tarzan's favourite Christmas song which is 'Jungle Bells'.

7 True. If you don't believe me you can visit his grave. Saint Nicholas died in Myra but seven hundred years later some Italian merchants attacked the monks who guarded his grave and saint-nicked his body. They took his body to Bari in Italy. He's Bari'd there now and his tomb is a shrine for Christians to worship at.

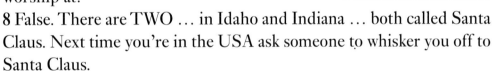

I WOULD LIKE...

8 False. There are TWO … in Idaho and Indiana … both called Santa Claus. Next time you're in the USA ask someone to whisker you off to Santa Claus.

9 False. In sixteenth-century France there was a 'secret' way of making tinsel (which was then called lamé). But in those days it was not used on Christmas trees but as decoration on soldiers' uniforms. Lamé was made by pulling copper wire through very small holes until the wire became as fine as human hair. It was then flattened by heavy rollers. The French lamé makers tried to keep their methods secret, but it soon leaked out to Germany, where it was used as the Christmas tree decoration we know as tinsel.

10 True. It was an old Kent custom to feed cockerels a bit extra on Christmas Eve. Then, if any evil spirits turned up, the cockerels would crow extra loud and scare them away. A special 'cake' of fat and flour

was baked into the shape of a corn sheaf and fed to the cockerels. That's still done today but it is fed to the ducks on Walmer pond instead of the cockerels. Maybe the ducks are expected to make a racket when evil spirits arrive? Real Christmas quackers!

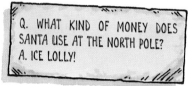

Q. WHAT KIND OF MONEY DOES SANTA USE AT THE NORTH POLE?
A. ICE LOLLY!

Score

10	Probably a sneaky Christmas cheat who looked at the answers. You're the sort of person who sneaks a look at their presents hidden in their parents' wardrobe.
7, 8 or 9	You're the sort of kid that your classmates probably hate to bits because you're usually top of the class and teacher's pet. Yeuch.
4, 5 or 6	Could do better – have you done all your Christmas revision?
1, 2 or 3	You are seriously unlucky. You're the sort of person who goes to see Santa and falls off his knee.
0	What a cracker you are. It's very hard to get this score!

CHRISTMAS CARDS

Christmas cards have made millions of pounds for printers and post offices and card shops. Here's a card from one of those irritating teachers who can't resist trying to fit some teaching in with the message! She has taken out some of the words and stuck them to the bottom of the card. But can you replace the words in the right places so it makes sense?

Happy Christmas to all my pupils!

Do you know how Christmas cards started? The first cards were printed for a businessman called Sir Henry (1) ...... in 1843. Sir Henry was a generous man and also gave the English people their first public (2) ......

He asked an artist to design a (3) ...... for him and 1,000 cards were printed. The spare cards were sold by the printer but they were a bit unpopular because they had a picture of a (4) ...... on the front.

Christmas cards became really popular when the penny post was invented. The most common picture was of a (5) ...... because postmen wore red jackets and that was their nickname. (They stopped wearing red in (6) ...... because red showed the (7) ......)

In the USA a miserable head (8) ...... tried to limit the number of cards that one person could send. He said his men were (9) ......

Nowadays charity Christmas cards are popular. The first charity card was drawn by a seven-year-old girl in (10) ......

lots of love,
Ms Drome

Missing words: muck, picture, 1861, overworked, Cole, pub, postmaster, toilet, 1949, robin

67

Did you Noel …?

John Horsley, the artist who drew that first Christmas card, later became famous for something else – he started a campaign to stop artists using nude models! He said it was disgraceful and shocking and rude. As a result John Horsley got a new nickname – Clothes-Horsley. (Clothes-horse … Clothes-Horsley, geddit? Oh, please yourself.)

Crazy cards

The Victorians took to Christmas cards like a reindeer takes to Christmas pudding. They loved them. Soon they were coming up with new ways to amuse their friends at Christmas.

Some of these bizarre Victorian card ideas included:

• a five pound note • a slice of bacon • an extracted tooth • a luggage label • roast mice!

I'm dreaming of a White Christmas

Christmas and snow. You can see the white stuff on your Christmas cards … but not outside your house on Christmas Day. The Victorians created the Christmas cards with snow and we've been stuck with them ever since. The Victorians had more white Christmases than we do today because they lived through a little ice-age.

But how many white Christmases did London have in the 20th century?

a) 2
b) 7
c) 13

Did you Noel …?

An old British superstition goes like this …

*If Christmas Day be bright and clear
There'll be two winters in the year.*

Cheerful! A sunny Christmas and you'll pay for it with two spells of seriously bad weather. Look on the bright side – two spells when the roads are too bad for you to get to school … or the school heating breaks down and you have to stay at home anyway! So a white Christmas is all right but a bright Christmas may be better!

Q. WHAT HAPPENS IF YOU SLIP IN THE SLUSH?
A. YOUR BOTTOM GETS THAW!

CHRISTMAS PUDDING

Look at your supermarket shelves at Christmas. They have all sorts of Christmas puddings, but a lot of them call themselves 'traditional'. Hah! Punch those puddings to a pulp and shout at the shop assistants, 'What a load of frumenty!' As they take you away to lock you up you can explain.

You want a real old Christmas pudding? Then get out the porridge.

In the Middle Ages the Christmas treat was spicy porridge – frumenty. (The medieval mush-makers used boiled wheat but you can use porridge.)

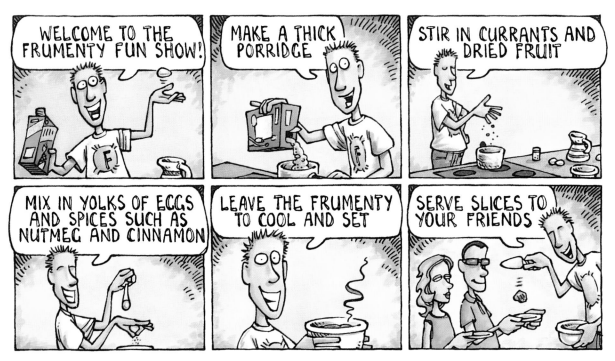

That's traditional. In some parts of Scandinavia this porridge is still a part of the Christmas dinner. Yucky, eh?

You may prefer to stuff yourself on this Georgian recipe. This is what most of us think of as 'traditional':

King George I's Christmas pudding 1714

10 eggs	1lb sugar
1½lb shredded suet	1lb breadcrumbs
1lb dried plums	1 teaspoon mixed spice
1lb raisins	1 teaspoon grated nutmeg
1lb mixed peel	½ pint milk
1lb currants	½ teaspoon of salt
1lb sultanas	the juice of a lemon
1lb flour	a large glass of brandy

Let the mixture stand for 12 hours. Then boil for 8 hours and boil again on Christmas Day for 2 hours. The mixture will give 9 pounds of pudding.

And George I should know – his nickname was what?
a) The Great Pudding Face
b) The Christmas King
c) The Pudding King

Answer:
c) Though **a)** might have suited fat Georgie too.

But is his pudding recipe too rich for you? Do you still prefer your local supermarket 'traditional' pudding?

Here are some of the ingredients printed on the wrapping of a Christmas pudding bought in a supermarket today:

"INGREDIENTS: DRIED EGG, SOYA FLOUR HOMOGENIZED MILK, MIXED DRIED FRUIT, CARAMEL COLOURING, MONOSODIUM GLUTAMATE, FLAVOURING, PRESERVATIVES"

Scrummy! Don't you just love that monosodium glutamate?

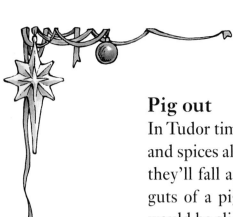

Pig out

In Tudor times Christmas puddings would be a mixture of meat, oatmeal and spices all boiled together. But if you just drop the ingredients in a pot they'll fall apart, won't they? What did they wrap the pudding in? The guts of a pig, of course. The pudding came out like a fat sausage and would be sliced and served with the boar's head. Tasty, eh?

A hundred years later Christmas puddings had changed. They were made with prunes (dried plums), boiled in a bag and served after the meat.

There is a story of how the boiled-bag mixture was first invented … but you don't have to believe it!

One Christmas Eve, an English king found himself deep in a forest with only a little food for his journey. He knocked on the door of a poor woodman's cottage and asked, 'My good man, can you offer me and my servant food and shelter?'

'Who are you then, fatty?' the woodman asked.

'I am your king and if you don't watch your lip I'll have your head served up for Christmas dinner!' the king told the man.

'Oooops!' said the woodman. 'I only have a little food, Your Majesty, Sir, Your Grace, Your Highness. Just some chopped suet, flour, eggs and a little ale.'

'Never mind,' the king's servant said. 'We have some apples, dried plums, sugar and brandy. Let's mix them all together.'

'Sounds disgusting!' the woodman thought but didn't dare say.

The result was a very gooey mixture. This sticky mess was boiled in a cloth, and served to the king. 'Amazing!' said the king.

'Tasty!' agreed the servant.

'Who'd have believed it,' said the woodman.

And the Christmas fruit pudding had been invented!

Stir-up Sunday

There was an old custom that everyone in a family took their turn at stirring the Christmas pudding. While they did it they each made a secret wish. This would also bring luck for the following year. The pudding was made the Sunday before Christmas and that day was known as Stir-up Sunday.

Why was it called Stir-up Sunday? Well that Sunday is usually the one nearest to Saint Andrew's Day. It was called 'Stir-Up Sunday' because in the prayer book for that day it says,

 'Stir up, we beseech Thee, O Lord, the will of thy faithful people.'

Pudding puzzler

Here's a game for those of you bored with television on Christmas Day. (Yes, in other words, a game for everyone!)

It's a game for two or more.

See how many questions you can get right. The person with the best score is the winner and gets the pudding. (If two or more people get the top score, they have to share.) The loser gets brandy sauce poured on his or her head (but put newspaper on the floor first to protect the carpet).

Pudding puzzler

1. An English law of 1551 says everyone must go to church on Christmas Day on . . . ?
a) Foot
b) Fire
c) Their best behaviour

2. Old Christmas Play performers (mummers) in Philadelphia USA, call themselves 'Two Streeters'. Why?
a) Because they come from a certain two streets in the city.
b) Because they perform in only two streets and nowhere else.
c) Because they come from 'Second Street' in the city.

3. The American National Christmas tree is where?
a) Central Park, New York, where 10 million people can see it.
b) King's Canyon in California, where about 10 people can see it.
c) Alaska, where about 10 polar bears can see it.

4. Victorian postmen were nicknamed 'Robins' because of their red uniforms. But why were their uniforms red?
a) So they could be seen in the snow and not run over by stage coaches.
b) Because it was the 'Royal Mail' and red was a royal colour.
c) So that if they were attacked and robbed the blood wouldn't show.

5.What did the Victorians use a goose club for?
a) It was a nail-studded lump of wood used to club geese to death.
b) It was a 'lonely goose' club to bring together unmarried geese.
c) It was a savings club.

6. Sherlock Holmes had a Christmas adventure called 'The Blue Carbuncle'.
Where was the blue carbuncle (diamond) found?
a) Inside a Christmas goose
b) Inside the sack of a burglar who disguised himself as Santa
c) Inside the pipe of his assistant, Doctor Watson

7. What was the poem 'The night before Christmas' called when it was first written?
a) 'A visit from Rudolf'
b) 'A visit from the Christmas fairy'
c) 'A visit from Saint Nicholas'

8. The Dutch Santa is dressed as a bishop and rides through the sky on what?
a) A reindeer
b) A horse
c) An angel

What's a pirate's favourite letter?
R

Answers:

1a) And it is *still* the law. So if you go to church on your new Christmas bike you ought to be punished – probably some old English punishment like having to sit through a five-hour sermon while your Christmas dinner gets cold.

2c) Twenty clubs still meet in Second Street and perform every New Year's Day. They don't all perform the same sort of play because that would be boring. There are the Comics (who don't go around reading comics), the Stringbands (who do go around playing music but not in string vests) and the Fancies (who wear enormous fancy-dress costumes).

3b) It's not a chopped-down fir tree, it's a living giant sequoia called The General Grant Tree. It's almost 100 metres high. (Hope the Christmas fairy on the top isn't afraid of heights!) Christmas trees don't have to be fir trees. In India, Christians decorate banana trees at Christmas.

4b) Must have been confusing if you were a 'Robin' called Robin!

5c) By saving a little each week they had enough to buy a goose to eat on Christmas Day.

6a) Wonder if the goose was killed with a goose club? And did it swallow the blue carbuncle before or after it was dead? You'll have to read the story to find out. Sherlock lets the thief go free because it's Christmas.

7c) ''Twas the night before Christmas and all through the house – not a creature was stirring, not even a mouse.' A bloke called Clement Moore wrote the poem for his family and a few friends. One of the friends sneaked a copy and sent it off to a New York newspaper. They published it and it became famous. Wonder if Clement paid his friend for doing that favour?

8b) If the horse is female then it must be a nightmare. Geddit?

CURIOUS CHRISTMAS CUSTOMS

There are hundreds of tall tales about Christmas customs. From not-so-jolly holly to miserable mistletoe. They're berry interesting.

Christmas trees

One of the stories of why we have Christmas trees says it started with the pagans in Germany who worshipped the oak tree. When Christianity arrived they still wanted to worship a tree so the priests suggested the pine tree – it's a triangle shape, with each point standing for the Christian 'Trinity' of the Father, the Son and the Holy Spirit.

For luck you should decorate your Christmas tree with …

- A spider and a web (Lithuania – from a legend that said a poor woman had nothing to decorate her tree with. Her children woke on Christmas morning to find it covered in glittering webs.)
- Straw birdcages (Lithuania – maybe for the spiders when they've done their web-making?)
- Painted egg shells (Czechoslovakia – just for a yolk, I guess.)
- Popcorn (America – streamers were made from popcorn dyed bright colours and laced on a string with nuts and berries. Berry pretty.)
- Horns and bells (Meant to make a noise and scare away any evil spirits.)

Scaring away spirits is also the idea behind putting an angel on the top. But what good is a Christmas fairy supposed to be? Does it scare away pixies?

Q. WHY IS A CHRISTMAS TREE LIKE A BAD TAILOR?
A. BECAUSE THEY BOTH KEEP DROPPING THEIR NEEDLES!

Dangerous decorations

In December 1867, American Charles Kirchhof invented a candle-holder with a weight on the bottom to help the candle stand upright. The problem was that the weight often caused the candle to slide off the branch – which was just as dangerous. The invention was not a great success.

In 1879 another American, Frederick Artz, invented a candle-holder with a spring clip that could be attached to the branch. It was made of tin, with a little cup at the bottom to catch melted wax. This type of holder became very popular and can still be bought today.

Victorians cleverly made their candles spiral. If a smooth-sided candle leans, the wax will run down on to the floor. With a spiral candle, this won't happen because the wax will run down through the grooves without dripping.

Even with these inventions, terrible accidents could happen. One American newspaper report dated 25 December 1887 described a fire in Matrawan, New Jersey:

Christmas was a joyous one in the home of Mr Robert Morris ... until this evening. Shortly before six this evening Mrs Morris decided to light the candles of her Christmas tree, which stood in the front room. Frank Morris, her six-year-old son, was close beside her as she with matches touched one candle then another. Frank became over-anxious, and seizing hold of a branch of the Christmas tree to see whether one of the candles was alight, he upset the tree. In an instant the whole tree was on fire. The tree in falling set fire to the house, and also to the clothing of Frank. When it was discovered that Frank's clothing was ablaze an attempt was made to put out the fire on him. It was too late, however ... The house was also burned down, causing a loss of about $500.

Most people had a special present under the tree – a bucket of water!

Did you Noel …?

In the town of Oberammergau in Germany Christmas trees are stuck on graves and lighted with candles so the corpses can join in the celebrations!

The yule-log

The pagan Celts believed the sun stood still for 12 days at the end of December when the days had grown shorter. If they could set fire to a log and keep it burning for those 12 days then the sun would decide to return and the days would grow longer. If your yule-log goes out then you'll have terrible bad luck – evil spirits can enter the house when the light goes out and the powers of darkness will swallow you. Did you also know …

- In Victorian England the log only had to burn for 12 hours, not 12 days – much easier.
- Other countries in Europe make it even easier by having a red candle burning for the 12 days.
- In Germany the ash from the log was kept all year round to protect the house from lightning – a shocking idea.
- In Scandinavia people believed the yule-log warmed the ghosts of dead relations who popped home every Christmas Eve – they would even set an empty place at the Christmas dinner table for a ghostly grandma or a ghoulish grandad. It's enough to put you off your pudding!

Q. WHAT IS A FOOTBALL SUPPORTER'S FAVOURITE CHRISTMAS SONG?
A. YULE NEVER WALK ALONE!

Holly

Why do we have the holly branches around our houses and on our Christmas cards at Christmas? There are plenty of strange explanations. Take your prickly pick:

1 There's an old story that a holly tree stood outside the stable where Christ was born. The battered bush had no berries, because the birds had eaten them all. As soon as Christ was born the tree burst into buds, flowers and berries, all in one night!

2 One legend tells how, after the birth of Jesus, the shepherds who went to visit the baby left behind a lamb. To keep it safe, and to protect it from wolves, they put the lamb in a pen made of prickly branches. But the lonely lamb was desperate to follow them back to its mum. It forced its way through the prickles which cut and tore its coat. As it was a cold night, the drops of blood froze on the prickles, and this is why holly has bright red berries!

3 Jesus was crowned with thorns. Holly is pretty prickly and the story went around that the red berries are the blood of Jesus. So you end up with holy holly.

Did you Noel ... ?

The holly and the ivy sung about in the Christmas carol stand for man and woman – tough holly men and clinging ivy women. The one that comes into the house first will be boss for the following year. So if holly comes across the doorstep first then the man will be head of the house. And it's bad luck to bring holly or ivy into the house before 24 December. Not a lot of people know that!

Mistletoe madness

Kissing under mistletoe comes from the days of the Druids before Jesus was even born.

The Druids held their mid-winter festival around the end of December. For a real un-Christian Christmas, gather your mistletoe in a Druid procession ...

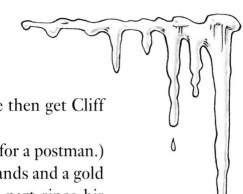

- First come the poets of the tribe. (If you can't find one then get Cliff Richard to sing 'Mistletoe and Wine'.)
- Then comes a herald – a messenger. (May be a good job for a postman.)
- Then comes the chief Druid in white robes with gold bands and a gold chain round his waist. (Your local vicar may like this part since his church will probably be empty.)
- Last come the peasants. (That's you!)

The chief Druid leads you into the woods to the sacred oak and uses a special gold knife to cut the mistletoe off the oak. He must catch it in the folds of his cloak – but not let it touch the ground. He will then pass it around to you peasants and bless you.

What's the use of that? Well, mistletoe is a healing plant, they say (unless you eat the berries and make yourself very, very sick). It will even heal a heart. If you meet an enemy under a tree carrying mistletoe then you are not allowed to fight!

If you carry mistletoe into someone's house they must give you shelter and protection – useful if you are being chased by next-door's rottweiler.

Where did all this kissy stuff come from? Maybe mistletoe was part of the Druid wedding ceremony. Certainly in northern Europe mistletoe was the symbol of Freya, the goddess of love. Her son was killed with an arrow tipped with mistletoe and her tears turned into the white berries. When he was brought back to life she kissed everyone who passed underneath the tree that was covered in mistletoe.

Any girl standing under mistletoe cannot refuse a kiss from a man … if she does, fellers, then recite the old verse:

It has been writ that any man
May kiss whatever girl he can,
And nobody shall tell him 'no'
Beneath the holy mistletoe.

… but beware, girls! If you stand there and *no one* kisses you then you'll go a year without love!

Superstition says you mustn't bring mistletoe into the house before 24 December ... and on Twelfth Night (6 January) it must be burned.

☠ HORRIBLE HISTORIES WARNING ☠

Remember coughs and kisses spread disisses. Do NOT kiss some strange person unless they have a note from their doctor showing they have all the right injections against swine fever, bubonic plague, mad cow disease and mad school disease.

Did you Noel ...?

In Scotland it was a New Year custom for a man to carry mistletoe into the house. He must be the first person to walk into the house in the New Year and should carry a piece of coal (which he puts on the fire), a coin (which he gives to someone in the family) and a sprig of mistletoe (which he puts on the mantelpiece).

Did you also Noel ...?

There is a legend that says Jesus was crucified on a cross made from mistletoe wood. After the execution the mistletoe tree shrivelled up with shame. That's why it has shrunk from a tree to the creeper you see today. A daft sort of superstition but many churches still refuse to have mistletoe in their Christmas decorations.

Wreally nice wreaths

Wreaths are usually seen at funerals. So why do people hang them on their doors at Christmas? Another old pagan custom from Scandinavia.

Evergreen branches were twisted round a wire hoop and four candles placed around the outside. The candles were lit and the wreath spun so the candles made a single circle of light – a magical sign that would drive away winter darkness.

When the Christians copied the wreath idea they began four Sundays before Christmas and lit one candle each Sunday.

Funny onions

Here's a Christmas custom you can try at home – all you need is an onion, some salt and a granny. It is a Swiss custom for forecasting the weather (useful if you want to know when to go to Blackpool for your holiday).

1 On Christmas Eve Granny cuts the onion in half and peels off twelve layers – one for each month of next year.

2 Each layer is sprinkled with salt.

3 On Christmas Day morning you must look at the layers. If the salt is dry then that month will be dry. If the salt is damp then that month will be rainy. Easy!

The bells

Before television and radio people were given news by the ringing of church bells. Just won a war? Ring out the bells! A new king is crowned? Ring out the bells. (A bit annoying if you're trying to get to sleep.)

In Scandinavia the bells ring out at 4:00 p.m. on Christmas Eve as a sign that Christmas has started and you can knock off work. (A bit like your school bell.)

In one English church in Dewsbury, Yorkshire, a very different kind of ringing is heard each Christmas Eve. The great bell rings as slowly as it does for a funeral.

Why? Who died at Christmas and is remembered in this way?

a) The Devil.

b) The vicar (back in 1762, who went up to ring the bells but fell off the bell tower and struck his head on a gravestone).

c) The vicar's girlfriend (in 1762, who sadly was playing Mary in a Christmas play at the time).

Answer:

a) That is because it used to be said that when Jesus was born the Devil sickened and died. So this bell, called the Devil's Knell, is rung during the minutes before Christmas. On the stroke of midnight all the bells ring out in joyful sound. Christ is born – evil and sin are conquered. Just imagine parents trying to get their excited kids to sleep and that racket starts! It's enough to make you move from Dewsbury!

Boxing Day boxes that weren't

Ask your teacher, 'Please, Sir/Miss/Monkey-features, do people have boxing matches on Boxing Day?'

Any old teacher will tell you Boxing Day (26 December) was the day when servants were given Christmas 'boxes' by their masters. But to really test your teacher, ask:

'Please, Sir/Miss/Monkey-features, what were Christmas boxes made of?' Then give them a choice of these three things …

a) wood

b) cardboard

c) clay

The answer is **c)** clay. And they were NOT made in the shape of a box! They were hollow clay balls with a slit in the top (rather like piggy banks).

And they were more pagan than Christian. These clay 'boxes' had been invented by the Romans for collecting money. The money went to pay for the winter festival food and drink. As it was a good money-grabbing idea it was borrowed by the Brits in Roman Britain.

On Boxing Day, servants used to go to their masters and ask for gifts of money. These 'boxes' had to be broken to get the money out. Country servants often called these boxes 'piggies'.

BET THEY HAD A SMASHING TIME ON BOXING DAY! HEH! HEH!

Boxing Day in church was when the priest opened the money boxes at the church door. (You can't expect to get into a church for free.) The money was used to help the poor and needy – if they were lucky. It ended in a priest's pocket if they weren't. Another name for Boxing Day used to be Offering Day.

Wet wassails

Do you live on a farm? (Or do you have a garden tree you want to grow well next year?) Try this old custom on Twelfth Night to make sure you have a boom in blooms. You need:

- Ale
- Stones or a shotgun

Now off you go into the garden and say to every tree:

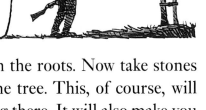

Apples and pears and right good corn,
Come in plenty to every one,
Eat and drink good cake and hot ale,
Give Earth to drink and she'll not fail.

Take a sip of drink, then scatter some ale on the roots. Now take stones and throw them through the branches of the tree. This, of course, will drive away all the evil spirits that were lurking there. It will also make you a bit unpopular with neighbours who have greenhouses.

Farmers also scattered ale on their corn to make it sprout. (You may like to try this on your cornflakes, but don't hold your breath and wait for them to grow.)

After guns had been invented they were fired through the trees as well as stones.

CHRISTMAS FIRSTS

You may think that we've been doing the same boring things every Christmas for thousands of years. Don't you believe it! You'd be amazed at how new some Christmas 'traditions' are … and at some of the weird things that have first happened on Christmas Day.

1 In 1841 Gateshead on Tyneside has a colourful first. What?
a) A white Christmas when snow fell two metres deep.
b) A blue Christmas when people turned blue as a result of a cholera infection.
c) A red Christmas when a local brickworks exploded and covered the town in brick dust.

2 In 1932 King George V gives the British public its first what?
a) Christmas message.
b) Christmas street-lights which he switched on at Chelmsford.
c) Christmas firework display from Buckingham Palace.

3 In 1800 there is a famous first at Windsor, where Queen Charlotte has what?
a) A Christmas tree.
b) A Christmas tree with electric lights.
c) A Christmas tree with woodworm.

4 In 1880 so many Christmas cards are being sent the Post Office makes its first plea to the public to what?
a) 'Post early for Christmas.'
b) 'Do not waste post office time. Do not send cards.'
c) 'Deliver your own Christmas cards and save the postman's feet.'

5 A legend from the Middle Ages tells of a little girl in Bethlehem who had nothing to give the baby Jesus. An angel took pity on her and gave her the first what?
a) Miniature angel to stick on Jesus' Christmas tree.
b) Christmas wrapping paper to wrap around the baby and keep him warm.
c) Christmas rose.

6 Christmas tree electric lights are first used in America around what year?
a) 1850
b) 1880
c) 1920

7 In 1914 Britain has a Christmas present from Germany that is a first. What?
a) The first German shepherd dog as a present for the queen.
b) The first German measles, caught by a Welsh boy in Scotland.
c) The first German bomb.

8 In 1841 there is the first mention of what?
a) Reindeers pulling Santa Claus across the sky.
b) Christmas crackers.
c) Balloons for Christmas parties.

9 In 1864 a club arranged what seasonal shivering fun first?
a) Taking off their clothes and racing to the top of Ben Nevis mountain in Scotland.
b) Taking off their clothes and sledging down the hill at Windsor Castle.
c) Taking off their clothes and swimming in a lake in London's Hyde Park.

10 In 1848 the magazine *Illustrated London News* publishes an extra 16-page section. The first what?
a) Christmas magazine special.
b) Christmas joke book.
c) Christmas recipe book.

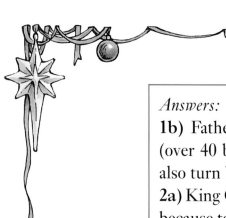

Answers:

1b) Father Christmas brought cholera to Gateshead. The victims (over 40 by Boxing Day) vomit and poo till they die painfully. They also turn blue. The disease is usually caught from infected water.

2a) King Georgie broadcast a message to the British people on the radio because television hadn't been invented. He spoke from Sandringham but he didn't say what he thought – his speech was written by popular poet Rudyard Kipling. A poet! What did he say? 'At Christmastime my wife and I, hope you have a nice mince pie.' Monarchs still bore Brits stiff with a Christmas speech but since 1957 they have taken over the television too – so now we have to look at them as well!

3a) Well it was the first tree in *Britain* – Charlotte probably brought the idea from her home in Germany where they'd had Christmas trees for a thousand years. She probably said to mad King George III, 'We'll stick a pine tree up!' and Georgie probably said, 'What fir?' A doctor Watkins was there and described Charlotte's tree, put up for the children of the palace workers:

In the middle of the room stood an immense tub with a yew tree placed in it. From the branches hung sweetmeats, almonds, and raisins in papers, fruits and toys. It was all illuminated by small wax candles. After everyone had walked around and admired the tree each child was given a few of the sweets and a toy. They all returned home quite delighted.

Just as well they didn't catch their clothes on the candles or they'd have gone home quite alighted.

The idea didn't catch on till Queen Victoria's husband (Albert – another German) had one put up 40 years after Charlotte's lonesome pine. Albert wrote to his dad …

Today I have two children of my own who are full of happy wonder at the German Christmas tree and its shimmering candles.

4a) In 1871 a miserable newspaper was complaining that Christmas cards filled the post offices and held up important business letters (e-mail hadn't been invented). By 1873 the first adverts were appearing in the newspapers saying: 'Mr & Mrs Blank will NOT be sending cards this year but wish all their friends a Merry Christmas'.

5c) The girl was called Madelon, it's said. She was on the snow-covered hills and the angel brushed away the snow to uncover a beautiful rose. Her gift to the baby was a flower … one that she'd ripped out of the ground and killed! There *is* a Christmas rose that grows in Europe and flowers in winter.

6b) In true Christmas spirit people get into nasty arguments and can't agree on when the very first lights appeared. Some say Ralph Morris used them first in 1895. But it seems the General Electric company say they had them in 1882. You want to argue? You want a Christmas knuckle sandwich? Whichever it is, answer **b)** is the closest, so shut up and get on with the next question.

7c) The first ever bomb to land on British soil was dropped by a German airship.

8b) Crackers were mentioned in a story that was published in June 1841. But there are no pictures of crackers till 1847.

9c) The Serpentine swimming club started Christmas swims. Why? Maybe you'd like to try it and find out – if you are as nutty as a Christmas walnut whip, that is.

10a) There *were* recipes and jokes in it. But there was also an attack on the way Christmas had become just an excuse for making money! A crusty character complained, 'Thirty or forty years ago people knew it was Christmas without being told so by an advert.' There are still people around saying the same thing today, over 150 years later!

THE KNIGHT BEFORE CHRISTMAS

What was the very first ghost story told at Christmas? It was about King Arthur and his knights of the round table. The old story says it was Christmas time in King Arthur's court at Camelot. Arthur and his knights and their ladies were enjoying their feast …

'Ooooh! He's lovely that Sir Gawain!' Greta the serving girl sighed. She was thin as the east wind that whistled through the castle corridors.

Her pudgy friend, Freda, frowned. 'You're drooling all over that Christmas pudding!' She was sweating with the work of serving at the round table in front of the blazing log fires.

Greta wiped her mouth with the back of her hand and rubbed the top of the steaming pudding with her grubby sleeve. 'Sir Gawain is

the greatest, bestest knight in the whole world, they say. Even better than Sir Galahad, or Sir Lancelot, or King Arthur himself.'

The knights weren't talking. They were too busy crunching on the bones of roasted swans and tearing at baked thrush pie at their Christmas Eve feast. They threw the bones on the rushes on the floor for the shaggy hounds to eat.

'I'm bored,' Freda sniffed. 'Nothing exciting ever happens here!'

'You shouldn't say that!' Greta gasped. 'Camelot's a magical sort of palace. Things HAPPEN! Especially at Christmas time.'

'What sort of things?' Freda sneered.

'Magical things. Anything can happen at Camelot! It's a lottery!' Greta whispered.

'A Camelot-tery!' Freda cackled.

But, no sooner had she said it than there was a roar of icy air that blew open the great doors. Knights froze with fear, their fists full of food. Ladies squeaked and squawked and all eyes turned towards the doors. There was the clatter of iron hooves on the stone floor and a green horse appeared. On its back sat a huge knight in green armour, a giant of a man. He raised the front of his helmet. His skin, his long hair and his bushy beard were a ghostly green colour. The giant wore a great fur-lined coat over his armour. In one hand he carried a bunch of holly, in the other an enormous axe.

The knight spoke, 'I am the Green Knight!' he roared. His voice sent the dogs running for cover under the huge round table and blew the yule logs into fierce flames.

No one said a word but Freda muttered, 'THERE'S a surprise!'

'I challenge the bravest knight to a Christmas game!' he laughed and his laugh boomed like a bell of doom.

'What game?' King Arthur asked. No one had ever heard the great king speak so weakly.

'A chopping game. Your bravest knight and I will chop each other's heads off! Who is brave enough to stand against me?'

Arthur cleared his throat. 'What are the rules, old chap?'

The green man grinned. 'Your knight can have the first blow. If I survive, I must be allowed to return the blow one year and one day from today.

Greta nodded, 'Sounds fair enough to me! Why, even I could win a fight like that!'

Freda shook her head. 'There'll be a catch, you wait and see!' She was so RIGHT!

Handsome Sir Gawain rose to his handsome feet and spoke in his handsome voice. 'I accept your challenge!'

Freda sighed, 'Poor Sir Gawain!'

The mighty round table was quickly cleared. 'Right, lads, lift it when I say "three",' Arthur ordered. 'Three!' he said suddenly and Galahad (who shared a brain with a turnip) almost fell over.

The green knight jumped down from his horse. He knelt among the cracked bones and the dog droppings and handed his axe to Gawain. 'Strike!' he ordered.

Gawain spat on his hands ... well, they were a bit greasy with all that swan fat ... and grasped the great green weapon. The giant knight lowered his green head and pulled his thick green hair away from his great green neck. Gawain gave a cry that would curdle blood – even green blood. 'Aiiieeee!' In one movement he raised the axe and brought it down with a whoosh.

'Bull's-eye!' Arthur cried as the great green head fell with a crunch to the floor. Blood spurted out of the naked neck. But the cheering knights soon fell silent when they saw that the green-furred body didn't topple.

Slowly the green arms reached out and fumbled over the rushes. At last they found the fallen head, gripped it firmly by the ears

and picked it up. The hands placed the head carefully back on the neck and the green lips parted to show grim green teeth.

The giant knight rose and gently took his axe from the trembling (but handsome) hand of Gawain. 'I'll be back,' the man said. He mounted his horse, clattered down the corridor and was gone as mysteriously as he'd arrived.

Freda chewed her knuckles. 'I told you so!'

'You did,' her thin friend agreed. 'But a lot can happen in a year and a day!'

And little Greta was right too! The next year, on Christmas Day, the knights gathered in the crowded room. It seemed like half of Arthur's kingdom had gathered to see the second leg of the contest. Greta and Freda could hardly get to the table for nosy nobles and prattling peasants, bug-eyed bishops and squint-eyed squires.

Arthur hammered on the table for silence and cleared his throat. 'Since we met here last Christmas Eve our great Gawain has not been idle!'

Queen Guinevere tugged at her husband's sleeve. 'Great and HANDSOME Gawain,' she reminded her husband.

'Ahem! Exactly! Gawain set out to find the lair of the giant knight … and he succeeded!'

'Of course he did,' Greta grinned. 'Heroes are good at that sort of thing!'

'He met the Green Knight's wife! The woman fell in love with him … because he's so good and handsome.'

'Can't say I blame her,' Greta sighed.

'He's as handsome as the next man – in a dark dungeon with dirty windows on a dingy day,' Freda agreed.

Arthur went on, 'And the Green Knight's wife gave him a belt …'

Freda chuckled, 'I'd give a strange knight a belt if he came calling on me when my man was away from home. A belt around his cheeky ear-hole!'

'Shush!' Greta hissed.

'A green silk belt!' Arthur explained. 'So long as he wears it he cannot be killed!'

'That's good,' Greta smiled.

'Yes. No blood for us to mop up because I'll bet we'd have got the job. We get all the dirty jobs round here,' Freda sniffed.

Just then the door crashed open and the Green Knight burst in, on his green horse. The bishops and priests and peasants and squires couldn't rush away from him fast enough! They tried to squeeze themselves into the cracks between the stones of the hall's walls.

The giant spoke in a voice that made the dogs' tails fly between their legs. 'A year and a day is gone,' he roared. 'Step forward, Sir Gawain!'

The young knight was as pale as the giant was green. He stood and bowed his head. The giant raised the axe and just as he began to move it down Gawain jumped aside. 'The chicken!' Freda frowned.

'Did I flinch when you chopped my head last Christmas Eve?' the giant asked. Gawain shook his miserable (but handsome) head. 'Then stay still!' The giant's hands moved quickly and the axe sped towards Gawain's neck like a swallow swooping after a dragonfly. As it touched the neck he stopped the blade. It made a small nick in the knight's neck and blood spurted out.

But Gawain wasn't badly hurt. He looked at the Green Knight curiously. 'That was your one blow! You can't take another!'

'That's right,' the giant said. 'I've decided you are such a good knight I will spare you. I sent my wife to chat you up but you were too good to fall for her. That's why I didn't chop you the first time. But you did take her gift of a belt … and it's naughty taking gifts from married women, isn't it?'

'He's right you know,' Freda nodded.

Gawain hung his head and he blushed. 'I was wrong. I'll wear that belt as long as I live to remind me to behave myself!'

'That slice on your neck was your punishment. Now you are free to go. Good night, good knight!' the Green Giant laughed and spurred his horse out of the door with a clatter and a rattle of hooves.

Everyone seemed to have been holding their breath since the moment he'd ridden into the hall. Now everyone let out their breath with a sigh. The sigh turned to a cheer and the banners round the hall shook with cheering and laughter.

Greta grinned, pulled a plum from her pudding, then passed the rest round to the happy feasters. Freda nodded till her chins wobbled. 'That's a story to tell your grandchildren – when you have them, Greta!'

Greta looked proudly at her handsome hero. Her pale eyes sparkled. 'Ooooh! It is, Freda!' she said happily. 'Sir Gawain and the Green Knight! It's a Christmas Day to remember!'

Freda smiled. 'It's more than that! It's … it's TWO CHRISTMAS KNIGHTS!'

Answers to the Christmas bored game on page 42:
1a), 2b), 5a), 6b), 7a), 10a), 13b), 14a), 15b), 18b), 20a), 21b), 24a), 25b), 27a) It's spicy porridge. **28a), 29b)** The letters were written to the Tolkien children and were supposed to come from Father Christmas. They described his adventures at the North Pole. In fact their dad, J R R Tolkien, wrote the letters … the old fibber.

CHRISTMAS FUTURE

There you are! A book full of foul facts about the horrible Christmas season – so you can say 'Bah! Humbug!' to all that festive folly! No need to thank me. Because, of course, you don't need to make Christmas horrible for humans. They do it for themselves, don't they?

But here are two final terrible facts:

THIS CHRISTMAS OVER A BILLION PEOPLE IN THE WORLD ARE SURVIVING ON LESS THAN 70 PENCE A DAY

THIS YEAR ELEVEN MILLION CHILDREN WILL DIE IN POVERTY. OVER FIVE MILLION WILL DIE OF STARVATION

Horrible Christmas has always been a time of grasping and greedily getting, but the true spirit of Christmas is in the *giving*. Jesus said we should share what we have with people who don't have so much – and it is his birthday after all (sort of).

THAT'S OK MR SANTA YOU KEEP IT. I'VE GOT PLENTY ALREADY

Some people make Christmas a time for being friendly and helpful. Getting in touch with family and friends that are forgotten for too much of the year. You may find out that the best part of Christmas is about sharing and giving.

After all … it is Christmas.

Have a good one.